Gospel of Doubt

Gospel of Doubt

by

P.M. Burrows

The Pentland Press Ltd
Edinburgh • Cambridge • Durham • USA

© P.M. Burrows 1998

First published in 1998 by
The Pentland Press Ltd.
1 Hutton Close
South Church
Bishop Auckland
Durham

British Library Cataloguing in Publication Data.
A catalogue record for this book is available
from the British Library.

ISBN 1 85821 554 4

Typeset by George Wishart & Associates, Whitley Bay.
Printed and bound by Antony Rowe Ltd., Chippenham.

PREFACE

This book is the result of a television programme and a heart attack. The first of these was presented by A.N. Wilson and sought to justify his loss of faith in Christianity. It had the effect of leading me to read Prof. G. Vermes' book, *Jesus the Jew* — a fine, scholarly work. To my surprise, I thought many of his findings compatible with Christianity, and felt that someone should write a book or pamphlet demonstrating this view. I never imagined myself as doing so, but waited patiently for someone in the academic world to undertake the task.

Then came the heart attack, which I suffered during what should have been a routine bowel operation. The result was that I found myself not, as expected, in the ordinary surgical ward, but in the intensive care unit. It. seemed that all I could look forward to was a sedentary life, without country walks, bicycle rides or swimming. So how was I to pass my days? I felt no relish for an undiluted diet of light novels and television. Perhaps I could write the book myself. After all, I had learnt the techniques of historical research from the great M.P. Charlesworth; and I would not lack for leisure. So as I recuperated, I set to work.

Prof. Vermes' book is particularly illuminating with regard to Jesus' miracles of healing and the narratives of his birth. The historical problems involved in the latter have long been known to people in universities and to those trained for the Christian ministry. But it is knowledge that they have kept largely to themselves, not breathing a word of it to those in the pews. 'The

Gospel narratives about the birth of Christ are subject to serious doubt', an elderly cleric once said to me, 'but it is not wise to reveal this fact to a village congregation.'

This is an obscurantist policy, leaving adult congregations to continue life with a kind of Sunday school religion; and in the modern age it is both unwise and imprudent. It leaves the field clear to agnostics and sceptics, whose tongues are not tied. Thanks to radio and television, their words and arguments can be heard in the furthest countryside. The latest ideas in all subjects are soon brought from Oxford onto Channel 4. There is no need to read them in learned journals.

Even without such disturbing influences, people will begin to feel doubts and feel tempted to discard their childhood faith. The carol picture of 'angels from the realms of glory' all sprouting wings is too easily felt to be akin to fairy tale and dismissed accordingly. Then the rest of the faith may be discarded with it. There is a challenge here which the Churches should meet openly. 'I cannot praise a fugitive and cloistered virtue, that never sallies out and sees her adversary.' There is, in fact, a respectable intellectual case to be made for belief; and frankness can do no harm.

Besides the difficulties in the Gospel birth narratives, A.N. Wilson[1] also popularised the doubts that some scholars have raised about the Biblical accounts of Jesus' trial before the Sanhedrin. Few outside university or ecclesiastical circles would previously have been acquainted with the writings in question. But the cat is now out of the bag; and, for good measure, Mr Enoch Powell has now published a book that made headline news, suggesting that Jesus was never crucified at all, but stoned to death. Here again there is a need for a reasoned defence of the Gospel narratives, so far as possible in 'language understood of the people'.

In my preliminary reading I have come across two other topics which ought to be addressed. One is the work of New

Testament scholars on Jesus' parables. It transpires that some of these may have been gradually remoulded in the course of transmission, much in the same way that Plato is thought to have developed and extended the philosophy of his master Socrates. In neither case was there any deliberate infidelity practised or anything propounded contrary to the spirit of the master's teaching. But this book would not have been complete without a summary of these modern researches.

Another discovery, which I owe to a slim volume by Ian Wilson, was the new *Gospel of Thomas*. It is now 50 years since this was found in Upper Egypt. So it is surely time that it was made more generally known. Accordingly I print the full text with some brief comments on its possible significance. A full account would form a large treatise in itself.

In this way, like Herodutus of old, I have found my story 'looking for additions'. Another problem was the chapter concerned with the doctrine of the Atonement. The grand difficulty in it, that it seems to involve the immorality of vicarious suffering, was first mentioned to me when I had, perhaps prematurely, got into the sixth form at the age of fifteen. I supposed that it was probably impious to pursue that line of thought, and soon turned to more juvenile things. Now, somewhat bolder with age, I take up the matter again in what I hope will not be considered a blasphemous and iconoclastic manner. It is a hard question and one too easily put aside for a morrow that never comes.

In these various ways I have tried to give the general reader some idea of the present status of New Testament scholarship. It may well be a far from up-to-date account. Learned works pour from the presses thick and fast. The world of scholarship is like that of the Red Queen, where it takes all the running one can do to stand still. All that an amateur can do is to show the general lie of the land, so that the faithful do not worship in happy ignorance. Our aim, I am sure, must be the same as Oliver

Cromwell's, who wished every member of his army to 'know what he loves, and to love what he knows'.

This strategy of openness has dictated the style and manner of the writing. Most books on religion are too obviously committed on one side or the other, too obviously trying to persuade. Yet that kind of tone is calculated to deter rather than convince the sincere inquirer. What he seeks is a balanced account, fairly putting the points on both sides. This is something I have attempted to achieve, to maintain a detached and objective outlook, always giving the Devil his due.

That procedure is anyway forced upon one by the nature of the material. The more one reads and inquires, the more one finds obstacles placed in the path of reaching assured results. There is the matter of an inscription with the vital name missing; there is the doubt whether the Jewish authorities had, or had not, the right of execution; and there is the suspicion that in the Gospel prophecies of Jesus' second coming the text has been tampered with. It is uncanny how often one is frustrated in this way.

I had a layman's inkling of this situation forty years ago; and I remarked to a young cleric, who later became a cathedral dignitary, that it was odd how one could not fully satisfy oneself of the truth of Christianity either through history or science or philosophy. 'No', he replied, 'we are not intended to.' In my seventies now, I see the wisdom of this answer. Our doubts are the condition of our freedom. We need not be ashamed of them or find them unaccountable.

Readers must not turn to these pages in the hope of finding or attaining certainties. They are not to be found; or I at least have not found them. This is therefore the book of one doubting Thomas for other doubting Thomases in this world. Not that intellectual agnosticism need exclude spiritual assurance and moral commitment. It is still open for a doubting Thomas to follow Jesus. But only he himself can make the decision. All this book can do is to help him to make an informed one.

This work is more a journalistic scissors-and-paste affair than one of scholarship. The only item that might interest the academic world is a conjecture on the site of Joseph's original home (p. 155). However, for the sake of the more studious readers I have added notes to the chapters to enable them to check up on my assertions or to pursue matters further. For their convenience I have referred always to the excellent Penguin translation of Josephus' *Jewish War* as more likely to be found in local bookshops than the Loeb Classics. Such readers will know that the *New English Bible* or another modern version, like, say, *The Jerusalem Bible*, is a more accurate rendering of the original Greek text than is the old *Authorised Version*. However, I have generally preferred to quote from the latter as more familiar and memorable unless it is actually misleading. It is also what any of the Church's lost sheep who happen to pick up this book will expect. They should, however, be warned that *The Bible Designed to be Read as Literature* (to quote a pre-war title) is one thing, and the Bible for serious study quite another. For the latter a modern translation is essential – especially for following the argument in Paul's letters!

ACKNOWLEDGEMENTS

Among former authors I must gratefully mention my indebtedness to two of Prof. Vermes' books on Jesus. It is remarkable to find such an objective and sympathetic approach in a Jewish writer. My chapter on Jesus' teaching relies very heavily on books by the German scholar Jeremias and Norman Perrin with some important additions to my first draft inspired by Mr Enoch Powell's commentary on St Matthew. For the chapter on the Trial I have quarried in many fields but would like to pay special tribute to Paul Winter's seminal study for its many shrewd insights, even though I dispute his main thesis. My obligations to Ian Wilson have already been mentioned.

I must also express my gratitude to certain publishing houses for permission to reproduce some passages verbatim from the following works: Stace, W.T. *Religion and the Modern Mind* Copyright © 1952 by Princeton University Press; *The Standard Edition of the Psychological Works of Sigmund Freud,* translated and edited by James Strachey © 1974 Sigmund Freud Copyrights The Institute of Psycho-Analysis and The Hogarth Press; Smith, Morton. *The Secret Gospel* © 1974 Victor Gollancz; Robert M. Grant and David Noel Freedman. *The Secret Sayings of Jesus According to the Gospel of Thomas* © 1960 Harper Collins; *The Gospel of Thomas,* translated by Thomas O. Lambdin, in Robinson, J.M. *The Nag Hammadi Library* © 1989 Harper & Row and E.J. Brill, Leiden. I am especially grateful to the last, since I think it contributes a great deal to readers' consideration of Jesus' teaching for them to be able to refer to the complete text.

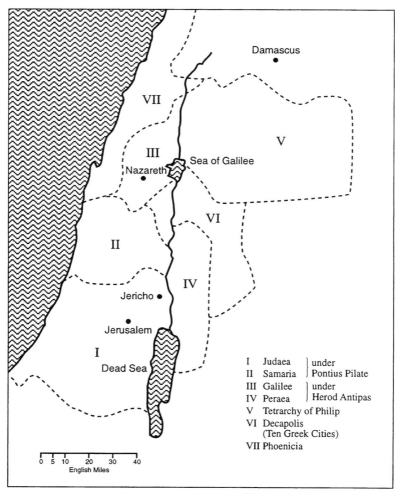

Damascus

VII

III

Nazareth

Sea of Galilee

V

VI

II

IV

Jericho

Jerusalem

I

Dead Sea

I	Judaea	} under
II	Samaria	} Pontius Pilate
III	Galilee	} under
IV	Peraea	} Herod Antipas
V	Tetrarchy of Philip	
VI	Decapolis (Ten Greek Cities)	
VII	Phoenicia	

0 5 10   20   30   40
English Miles

Palestine in the time of Jesus.

THE BACKGROUND

Jesus' homeland was what would now be called an occupied territory, having become part of the Roman empire in 63 B.C. It was, however, allowed a measure of self-government and was ruled from 38-4 B.C. by Herod the Great as client king. Client kings had something of the same status as the native princes in British India, except that there was no guarantee that sons or relatives would succeed them – as Britain's Boudicca learnt to her cost. The arrangement was a purely personal one between themselves and Rome. Indeed, they were almost expected to ripen their territories for annexation by promoting cultural convergence with the older provinces and Rome.

Herod proved himself a model vassal, introducing Graeco-Roman civilisation with enthusiasm. He rebuilt the former northern capital of Samaria under the name of Sebaste (Augusta), and did the same for Strato's Tower on the coast, which he rechristened Caesarea (rather as if war-torn Coventry had become Hitlerburg.) This latter had excellent harbour walls, traces of which can be seen today, and opposite the harbour mouth a temple of Caesar Augustus. The rest of the city too was in Roman style, with theatre, amphitheatre and forum. Herod also instituted four-yearly games on the model of the Olympics, named likewise after Caesar. His love of Greek athleticism seems to have been genuine. Besides financing the appointment of gymnesiarchs in neighbouring cities, he gave ample financial support to the Olympic games and presided over them once when on a journey to home.

1

This process of hellenization had, by Jesus' manhood, extended to mainly agricultural Galilee. Only four miles from his home in Nazareth lay the Graecised city of Sepphoris with a theatre holding 5000 and a population of 25,000. Jesus and his followers could probably speak Greek as well as their native Aramaic (Hebrew now being used only for sacred purposes.)

None of this programme endeared Herod to his Jewish subjects. Other subject peoples were quick to appreciate the benefits of imperial rule and to embrace its culture. Barbarous Britons were soon to study the art of public speaking. There was a very real ladder of opportunity, mainly through military service. Already by the end of the first century there was a Spanish emperor in Rome, and one of the Emperor Hadrian's leading generals was a Moor. But the Jews spurned these prospects. Their religion stood in the way. They held themselves apart.

Indeed, had they desired to blend in with the other, Gentile, races the process would have been fraught with obstacles. Social contacts were hampered by religious taboos. These forbade Jews the eating of pork; but this was the Gentiles' favourite food. A pig, wrote Pliny the Elder, had fifty different flavours imparted by cooking, whereas other animals had only one. More seriously still, a meal in a Roman household began with an offering to the household gods, and it was very possible that in the courtyard of a provincial's home would be a private shrine in honour of the divine emperor. This was more an indication of how Rome's subjects appreciated the benefits of the Augustan peace than a theological assertion. It meant little more than for a Victorian household to have a portrait of the Queen above the mantlepiece. But to the Jews this was anathema, a denial that Yahweh was the one true God. Satan and his angels, a Christian writer declared later, had penetrated every corner. The Jews remained irreconcilable.

Trying to face both ways, Herod began the building of a great new temple in Jerusalem. But his Judaism was never more than nominal, and he was so careless of religious proprieties as to have erected over its gate a golden eagle. This was a direct contravention of the Mosaic rule to have no graven images; and, knowing that the King's health was failing, two rabbis encouraged their students to remove it. Two ringleaders did so by having themselves lowered down from the roof on ropes, not secretly by night, but at midday in full public view. Herod exploded with rage and had the pair burnt alive and forty others executed.

He was equally ruthless against any suspected of disloyalty, not excluding members of his own family. He had executed or assassinated the two husbands of his sister Salome, his wife Mariamne, and three of his sons. It was, quipped Augustus, safer to be Herod's pig (*hus*) than Herod's son (*huios*). In extenuation it must be recorded that he was surrounded by such a web of intrigues and counter-intrigues as to make any man distraught. They were the natural result of mutually jealous wives, of whom Herod had ten.

He died soon after the affair of the golden eagle and, as one of Rome's favourites, was allowed to dispose of his territories by will. He named as his successor his son Archelaus, who inherited a situation that required careful handling. Instead he adopted crude, punitive measures, and these provoked the Jews to send a deputation to Rome actually begging for direct provincial government. Representations were also made by his brothers Philip and Antipas as rival claimants to the throne. The shrewd Emperor decided to resolve the issue by partitioning the country, awarding Judaea, Samaria and Idumaea to Archelaus, Galilee and Peraea to Herod Antipas, and the north-eastern regions to Philip.

Archelaus failed to profit by this second chance and actually contrived to unite the mutually hostile Jews and Samaritans against him. He was deposed in 6 A.D. and his realm made a minor Roman province under the rule of a procurator, subordinate to the governor of Syria. Religious affairs, however, were still left to the ordering of the High Priest and the Council of the Sanhedrin; and to the Jews religion would cover a very large area of life.

But the High Priest and the Council were like sparrows on a string. Law forbade the High Priest to summon the Council, and the Council to meet, except when wearing his state robes; and these were kept by the Roman governor. Moreover the High Priest was always his appointee. These two provisions ensured that the Jewish establishment would practise a Vichyite complaisance.

Meanwhile a body known as the Pharisees played rather the part of the Roman Catholic church in Poland during its successive partitions by neighbouring powers. It did much in those dark days to maintain the national consciousness and identity. And it did something of the same for the Irish during the eighteenth and nineteenth centuries. It was Catholicism that marked them off from the Protestant English and kept the national spirit alive. But it was not only a matter of preserving the Jews' national and cultural awareness. As with the Roman Church, this was only a by-product of the main activity. The Pharisees and their associates, the Scribes, had a larger vision and ideal. They believed that once the Mosaic code was observed by every Jew in all its fulness, the Kingdom of God would begin and a new age would dawn both for Israel and for the world.

This, however, was a particularly tall order. For, as the people's spiritual advisers, the Pharisees overplayed their hand in an excess of enthusiasm. Over the centuries the bare bones of the Mosaic code had been expanded with an oral tradition designed to give guidance in every life situation. In all 613 rules had been concocted.[1] A modern parallel would be the Roman Catholic catechism, which deals with a whole gamut of ethical problems, including the modern sins of tax-evasion and reckless driving.

The Pharisees had added so many refinements and minutiae that the working population were almost bound to offend against some ritual prescriptions because of the pressing demands of ordinary life. 'They bound heavy burdens and grievous to be borne, and laid them on men's shoulders.' Meanwhile in their leisure and high status, some Pharisees made a parade of their own holiness.

These are the Pharisees we hear most of in the Gospels. But there was also a moderate section led by Jesus' near contemporary, the Rabbi Hillel. And there was a developing counter-movement pressing for simplification of the Law. We get a glimpse of this in one of the Scribes' question to Jesus (Mark 12.28): 'Which commandment is the first of all?' No religious or political organisation is a seamless robe, uniform in colour and texture. And we have to remember this in reading the Gospel accounts. As late as 62 A.D. some Pharisees were giving Christians their support.

This is not surprising if we study *The Testaments of the Twelve Patriarchs*, a document written by a Pharisee between 109 and 107 B.C. Its ethical teaching, and even its phrasing, anticipates Jesus' Sermon on the Mount: 'Love ye one another from the heart; and if a man sin against thee, speak peaceably to him . . . and if he repent and confess, forgive him. . . . And if he be shameless and persist in wrongdoing, even so forgive him from the heart, and leave to God the avenging.' The Pharisees intended well, and as a body they had great prestige and were popular with the mass of the people. In Herod's day there were 6000 of them[2] in a country just slightly bigger than Wales. This means that they were thicker on the ground than Church and Chapel ministers combined in the Principality.

Little is known of the opposing group, the Sadducees, beyond what we read in the Bible – that, whereas the Pharisees believed both in the resurrection of the dead and in angels, the Sadducees denied both. A company of aristocrats, they agreed with the chief priests in favouring a policy of pragmatism and acceptance of Roman domination. The Roman empire included all the countries bordering the Mediterranean sea and was protected on the South by impassable deserts and on the North by the rivers Rhine and Danube. Its overthrow could not be envisaged on any sober estimate.

No such prudent thoughts appealed to the Zealots, a resistance movement that came into being on the Roman annexation of Judaea in 6 A.D. Before then the real loss of independence had been screened by the formal rule of Herod the Great. Now this was made visible by the presence of a Roman garrison in Jerusalem and by a census heralding taxation. Judas the Galilean raised the standard of revolt, asserting that the land belonged to God and that its taxation by foreigners was a sacrilege. Inevitably he and his freedom-fighters were suppressed; but his followers, the Zealots, continued to agitate and hope with a fanaticism born of failure and religion. They may be compared to Sinn Fein in Ireland. To such men benign government weighs little beside the symbols and emblems of sovereign nationhood.

Some time later there developed among them what the I.R.A. would call 'active units', the Sicarii or 'Dagger Men'. The name is Latin and a term coined by the Roman garrison. They strove to forward their cause by political assassinations, often in crowded gatherings, and were adept at melting away in the sympathetic multitude. Just when these activities began is unclear. The Jewish historian Josephus is not consistent with himself on the point. But agitators commonly become more extreme over time; and one would expect such violence to increase in the decade before the Jews' open revolt against Rome in 66 A.D. Josephus' later dating of the development, to about 50 A.D., is therefore to be preferred. The question is of some importance since suggestions have been made that Jesus' betrayer, Judas Iscariot, was a sicarius. The jumbled letters are the only evidence for the view; but other explanations of his name are to seek.

Another group, the Essenes, was briefly brought to the notice of the popular press soon after the last war by the discovery of the Dead Sea Scrolls; and some scholars saw a connection between them and Jesus' following. That opinion is now less fashionable, but has recently formed the basis of a sensationalist theory propounded by the Australian Dr Barbara Thiering in two books, *Jesus the Man* and *Jesus of the Apocalypse*. She argues that Jesus was no pacific preacher but a militant resistance leader who survived crucifixion through having his followers administer a drug to him in a wine-soaked sponge (cf p. 108 below) which gave the appearance of death, so that he could be taken down from the cross and revived, to carry on his underground work. He was not the bachelor figure of the Gospels but married Mary Magdalene and fathered a family. The Gospels, Dr Thiering believes, are almost deliberately misleading and are written in a code which it has been left for her, all these centuries later, to decipher.

Some of these suggestions, e.g. that Jesus was a Zealot sympathiser (see pp 90 below), have been made previously and dismissed by scholars. New are such identifications as that of Mary Magdalene with Jairus' daughter (whose raising from apparent death is said to be code for promotion within the sect), of John Mark with the centurion at the foot of the cross, of Jesus himself with the Dead Sea Scrolls figure of The Wicked Priest, and of John the Baptist with The Teacher of Righteousness. In general one can say that it is only when there are grave difficulties in taking an ancient text literally that one needs to explore further. But any who think that Dr Thiering's thesis should be taken seriously will find the issues involved ably dealt with by Dr N.T. Wright in his *Who Was Jesus?* The consensus of scholars is against her.

THE EVIDENCE

A biographer of Julius Caesar is in a fortunate position, having available to him the dictator's own campaign memoirs and the many letters of the contemporary politician Cicero. The latter often afford a dating of events to the exact month and day.

Anyone essaying to narrate the career of Jesus of Nazareth has no such advantage, it seems. The earliest relevant documents are the letters of the apostle Paul, running from 50 A.D., or some 20 years after Jesus' crucifixion; but these are mainly concerned with issues of ethics and theology – although containing two important references to the Resurrection and the Last Supper. The Gospel of John is commonly thought not to have been written before about 100 A.D., Mark's about 70 A.D. and Matthew's and Luke's about fifteen years later. It is commonly accepted that Luke was the author both of the third Gospel and of The Acts of the Apostles, as well as being Paul's travelling companion. But cautious scholars doubt whether the disciples Mark, Matthew and John were the authors of the works that bear their names. At that rate only Luke could be claimed to have lived at the time of the events that he describes; and even he would have been only a five-year old.

Nor can Mark, Matthew and Luke be regarded as independent witnesses. As compared with John's, their gospels all bear an obvious family resemblance to each other and view Jesus from the same angle – the reason that they are known as the Synoptic Gospels. Between the wars this similarity was accounted for by what is known as the Two-Source Hypothesis.

This claimed that Matthew and Luke had both relied on Mark for their narrative framework, even copying from him verbally in schoolboy fashion,[1] then added some items of their own and a great deal from a collection of Jesus' sayings. The existence of such a collection (known to scholars as Q from the German word Quelle, 'a source') is only an inference, but a fair one. A similar compilation, entitled *The Gospel of Thomas*, was discovered in Upper Egypt in 1945. The author of Matthew seems also either to have used, or himself amassed, a number of proof texts, designed to demonstrate that Jesus was indeed the Jews' promised Messiah.

The Two-Source Hypothesis is still accepted by most scholars, though with modifications. But it has recently been challenged by Mr Enoch Powell, who has, since his retirement from politics, been turning to New Testament studies and learning Hebrew for the purpose. He was a already a professor of Greek before the War, specialising in textual criticism; and as such he has proposed some convincing emendations of Matthew's text. 'Hiding one's light under a bushel' (Matt. 5.15) has always been a puzzling metaphor to those who reflect that a bushel measure looks much like a bucket. Enoch Powell shows how a slight change in the manuscript reading could give the much more intelligible 'footstool' for 'bushel'.[2] Another instance is Matthew 6.28, where 'they toil not, neither do they spin' should be revised to '*card* not etc.' (The first process after wool has been washed is the *carding*.)

A minute examination of the original Greek texts leads Enoch Powell to resurrect the early Church belief that Matthew's was the earliest Gospel, and that Luke was largely dependent upon it, often editing the language so as to make it more intelligible to his non-Jewish readership. He himself was obviously puzzled by the Hebrew word 'Mammon' (Matt. 6.24 and Luke 16.13). Sometimes he found Matthew's narrative itself puzzling in its implausibility, so ventured to make changes and additions to it so as to render it more inherently probable. Matthew (4.19, 20) gives no reason why Peter and Andrew should promptly have left their fishing nets and obeyed Jesus' summons to be his disciples. Luke (5.1), alone of the evangelists, supplies a motive for their response in the form of a miraculous draught of fishes. He is also alone in attributing to Jesus another miraculous feat. All the gospel-writers agree that when the soldiery came to arrest Jesus in the garden of Gethsemane, one of his followers struck at the High Priest's servant and cut off his ear. The only sequel in Mark, Matthew and John is a command from Jesus to refrain from violent resistance; but Luke has Jesus restore the severed ear. It seems odd that, if these miraculous events in fact occurred, the other writers should have failed to report them (Matt. 26.51, Mark 14.12-15, Luke 22.10).

It seems clear that Luke had Matthew's gospel before him as he wrote. In fact he virtually admits as much in his introduction. Matthew could have been one of the 'many writers' that preceded him. But Enoch Powell goes on almost to stand the Two-Source Hypothesis on its head, arguing that Mark wrote his gospel last of all with reference to Matthew's and Luke's. This is less convincing. Overall it might seem that Mark's work is an abridgement of the two former; but there are five narratives where Mark's account is longer and fuller than Matthew's;[3] and in one of these, where Jesus raises Jairus' daughter apparently from the dead, Mark alone gives the original Aramaic words with which he does so. Mark too is alone in reporting the healing of a blind man at Bethsaida (5.41 and 8.22). It is also difficult to understand why he should have omitted so much of the Sermon on the Mount and so many of Jesus' parables. A good reason, on the Two-Source Hypothesis, may be that he was not in Palestine when the document Q was composed and published. Enoch Powell's theory does not account for these facts.

One passage, however, is very much in his favour. In Matt.

3.11 the Baptist says, 'he that cometh after me is mightier than I, whose shoes I am not worthy to bear' (*Authorised Version. The New English Bible* replaces 'bear' with 'take off' – an impossible rendering of *bastazein*). Enoch Powell explains the phrase with reference to an Egyptian slate palette, on which King Narmer is shown barefoot and followed by a tiny sandal-bearer. This suggests that 'bear his sandals' was a traditional colloquialism for 'be his valet', and unfamiliar to Gentile readers. Similarly the old English 'boot-catcher', a term for an inn servant charged with relieving guests of their, perhaps muddy, boots, might have puzzled an American visitor in late Victorian times. The obvious conclusion is that the Greek Luke (3.16) substituted 'untie the shoelaces' so as to make the passage more intelligible, and was then followed in this by Mark (1.7), who for good measure added a 'stoop down'.

There is a complication, though. And that is that we cannot be sure that our present text of Mark is that penned by the original author. There was no law of copyright in the ancient world, and there was nothing to prevent some later writer from producing a 'new and revised edition' of a famous author's work without indicating his own additions and alterations. Enoch Powell shows how this was probably the case with Matthew's gospel; and it could equally well have been so with Mark's. There are clear signs of tampering in the eschatological chapter (see p. 81 below), and there could have been other modifications. All three Synoptic Gospels could have influenced each other as they developed. If so, two important conclusions would follow: (1) that the original drafts of our Gospels may have been made much earlier than supposed, and (2) that parts at least may have been written by the traditional authors. J.A.T. Robinson believes that there were 'proto-gospels', intermediate between missionaries' preaching notes and our fully developed Gospels.[4] From this viewpoint the investigation of sources is of more than academic interest. It may reveal that what Enoch Powell calls 'the underlying book' was composed not too long after the events it records.

This leads on to the thought that the underlying book of our existing Mark's gospel may have been the work of the John Mark to whose house Peter fled after his escape from prison (Acts 12.12), and who was taken by Paul on his first missionary journey. In two passages of his *History of the Church* Eusebius (c. 325 A.D.) reports that Mark made a record of Peter's reminiscences of Jesus' doings while the latter was preaching the Gospel in Rome.[5] J.A.T. Robinson thinks that this might have been in 42 A.D.; for it is certain that some apostle must have been engaged in missionary work there, since along with the Jews who were expelled from the city in 49 A.D. were the Christians Aquila and Priscilla (Acts 18.2). Alternatively Mark may have written his account when Peter returned to Rome after the Council of Jerusalem in 48 A.D., when the question of whether non-Jewish converts should have to face the rite of circumcision was debated. We know from Paul's letter to the Colossians (4.10) that Mark was with him during his captivity in Rome; and tradition has it that Peter suffered martyrdom there along with Paul in 64 A.D.

This story of Peter's end has been confirmed to some extent by archaeology. Beneath St Peter's, Rome a first century cemetery has been excavated, where the builder of a red wall obviously took special care to avoid disturbing a certain grave. This lies directly beneath the high altar of a previous basilica traditionally built above St Peter's tomb.[6]

So far this account of the origin of Mark's gospel is credible enough. The only doubt comes in Eusebius' remark that the source of his information, Papias, Bishop of Hierapolis (c. 140 A.D.) was 'a man of very mean capacity'. Otherwise the various references hang together well and do suggest that, contrary to first appearances, the Gospels are based on contemporary eyewitness.

It is also possible that the apostle Matthew may have laid the basis of the gospel named after him. Shorthand was not unknown in the ancient world, and speedwriters were employed by the consul Cicero to record a crucial debate in the Roman senate. Another example, yet to be deciphered, came from the Qumran caves, where the Dead Sea Scrolls were found. As a tax-gatherer and business man, Matthew would have had numerous occasions for, as well as the skill to make, rapid jottings. Again Eusebius quotes Papias as saying 'Matthew compiled the *logia* in the Hebrew language' (where *logia* means 'notable utterances' rather than 'oracles').[7] This suggests that Matthew himself compiled the document Q, the language of which shows traces of having been written originally in Aramaic. On the analogy of *The Gospel of Thomas*, this probably contained not only brief sayings but a number of parables.

Peter was not the only apostle who undertook missionary work and used his reminiscences by way of preaching. Thomas is credited by tradition with carrying the Gospel to Parthia, and even with proceeding from there to Southern India. This might explain how in 1501 the Portuguese found a Christian community already established in Malabar. And there would have been others, all relating separate incidents from Jesus' career as part of their evangelism. In the same way today sermons are preceded by a reading from one of the Gospels. It is easy to believe that the preachers would have kept some aides memoire to turn to before they addressed their congregations; and this would explain Christianity's preference for the codex or book form for its Gospels rather than the parchment scroll. In a codex the desired passage could be much more rapidly found.

This accounts for the modular character of the Gospels, which led between the wars to the development of Form Criticism. This sought to apply to the New Testament the methods of the scientific study of mediaeval folklore with its stock patterns and motifs. Observing that many Gospel incidents lead up to a quotable dictum, critics argued that only the saying itself is authentic, and the preceding narrative a subsequent invention designed to introduce it. On these lines some scholars declared that all that really survives from Jesus' ministry is forty original sayings.

This was obviously going too far. Details do indeed get added to stories in the telling, but the main point is not lost. And but for the constant telling and retelling of these tales, little of Jesus' career would remain known. Or how many of us can recall with accuracy the events of twenty years ago? During the North African campaigns of the last war we thought that the map of the area would stay forever engraved on our minds; but how many of those who lived then could re-draw it today? It was the apostles' constant preaching of the Gospel which kept the events of Jesus' life fresh in mind and is the best guarantee that the picture of him given in the New Testament is reliable.

On the other hand, because the gospels are a patchwork quilt of stories collected from various sources, with no two adjacent tales attributable to the same ultimate author, no two sections are necessarily equally worthy of trust. There is still need for historical judgment and acumen. We may credit a report of Jesus' cure of a case of mental derangement, and yet have doubts about his having walked upon water.

The Higher Criticism is on its strongest ground over the gospel attributed to John. The Jesus of this gospel seems to be a different person from the one portrayed in the other three. In them he is characterised by short, pithy utterances and maxims based on common life. Here he is given to long, sermonizing discourses. And these are very much alike in language and theology to the First Letter of John. The suspicion arises that it is only the incidents that provoke these speeches that are authentic, while the discourses that follow are attributable to the author. Sometimes, as in the case of Jesus' encounter with the Samaritan woman, both incident and discourse seem to have been invented.

Similar doubts arise over the philosophy of Socrates and Plato's development of it. Their theories form a continuum, so that it is not easy, when studying Plato's dialogues, to decide at which point Socrates becomes merely the mouthpiece of his famous disciple. There is the same problem with the teachings of the sage Pythagoras and the Pythagorean School. The latter clearly felt no compunction about publishing their own extensions of the founder's theories under his proper name. It lent them prestige; and in the ancient world disciples of a famous philosopher or thinker would have seen no dishonesty in the practice, but have rather regarded it as a higher fidelity or homage. But whatever the purity of the author's intentions, our awareness of this attitude of mind, as well as stylistic considerations, should make us cautious about using the Fourth Gospel as a historic text for Jesus' own thoughts and utterances. However, John's account of Jesus' last week is an independent version, and useful narrative details may be gleaned from it and from the gospel as a whole.

If caution is required in reading the gospel of John, even greater is called for in using *The Gospel of Thomas*, discovered at Nag Hammadi in Upper Egypt in 1945. It is quite distinct from another *Gospel of Thomas* which was already known of in the nineteenth century. The latter is no more than a collection of stories about Jesus' boyhood, and represents him as a youthful wizard who made clay sparrows fly, could lengthen pieces of wood, and brought a dried and salted fish to life. The more recently found work is a Coptic translation, made about 350 A.D., from a Greek original. This was written about 200 A.D. in Palestine or Syria; and a fragment of it was discovered at Oxyrhynchus in 1987.

The new *Gospel of Thomas* (see p. 21) is not a connected narrative, but a collection of disconnected sayings. Many of these are identical, or nearly identical, with those in the canonical gospels, e.g. 'You see the mote in your brother's eye, but do not see the beam in your own eye'; and several familiar parables, e.g. that of the Sower and the Grain of Mustard Seed, are reproduced – a valuable testimony to their authenticity, since it looks as if the *Gospel of Thomas* was composed independently of the Four Gospels. But there are also a number of sayings otherwise unknown, and generally couched in arcane and opaque language. What, for instance is one to make of the following?

> Jesus said to them, 'When you make the two one, and when you make the inside like the outside and the outside like the inside, and the above like the below, and when you make the male and the female one and the same, so that male be not male nor the female female, and when you fashion eyes in the place of an eye, and a hand in place of a hand, and a foot in place of a foot, and a likeness in place of a likeness; then you will enter (the Kingdom)'.

Gosp. Thomas No. 22

This riddling, allusive language and (No. 62) a reference to 'mysteries' have been thought to indicate that *The Gospel of Thomas* has been tampered with to fit in with what later became known as the Gnostic heresy. Gnosticism was a philosophy which regarded the world, not as created by God, but as wholly evil, and the soul of Man as an alien in it and a stranger. Salvation for him could come only through special insights and revelations vouchsafed to the elect by a divine saviour coming from elsewhere. This outlook was already present in Egypt in pre-Christian times, and seems to have coloured Egyptian Christianity when introduced. However, the Gospel of Thomas cannot simply be dismissed as a Gnostic text. It nowhere speaks of the material world as wholly and incurably evil. Moreover, the Gnostic heresy cannot have sprung out of nothing. Its existence provokes the question whether there was not something in Jesus' teaching that encouraged it. This, though, is better considered in a later chapter.

The challenge of the obscure language stimulated Hugh

McGregor Ross to spend eight years learning Coptic, the better to find the meaning of the text; and he has made an interpretation of it which is both plausible and explains much.[8] The central concept of this Gospel, he believes, is an anticipation of the Quaker doctrine of the Inward Light, and is reminiscent also of the Stoic idea of a divine spark in everybody and everything. We all of us have within us a portion of the Divine; but in most people this is overlaid and obscured by the self-assertive tendency of the Ego. This bias is something we do not have at birth ('Heaven lies about us in our infancy'); and there is no such thing as original sin (a notion that came in with Paul), but is an element which develops. It is self-regardant, assertive, self-opinionated, proud, and aggressive – that part of us appealed to often by television advertisements and glossy promotion brochures. Knowledge of the Truth can be won only by overcoming the dominance of this Ego; and once this is done, the true Self is revealed, and we also know God/the Light/the One/the All/the Kingdom/the Life (all synonymous terms), from which we originally have our being. Thus the Beginning is also the End. We can have eternal life here and now – there is no need for resurrection. In this way we can achieve an integrated personality ('make the two one'). But to gain this may involve being a 'loner'/solitary/*monachos* ('It is dissension which I have come to cast upon the earth' No. 16).

Rejection of the Ego is not the same as otherworldliness and asceticism. Nor is there any condemnation of sexual behaviour; and here *The Gospel of Thomas* is in line with modern thought. Perhaps also the above quotation (No. 62) is suggesting that the distinction between male and female is unreal – a sentiment echoed by Paul, declaring that in Christ 'there is neither male nor female' (Gal. 3.28). The saving knowledge, it is important to note, is not intellectual knowledge, but more like knowledge of a person. Perhaps, to use some words of Plato's, 'it flares up suddenly in the soul,' after, and as a result of, long discipline.

This approach sheds a great deal of light on a difficult document, and is acceptable in large part. But, of course, Thomas was not Freud; and the term Ego is an anachronism. In a way McGregor Ross' interpretation seems almost too plausible. The document begins by saying that 'These are the secret sayings which the living Jesus spoke', implying that they are for the elect and too difficult for the multitude. But Thomas' Gospel as paraphrased by him could certainly be understood by ordinary folk. If that is all there is to it, why did Jesus have to employ such abstruse and riddling language? The Stoics had shown how to make intellectual concepts intelligible to the common man with such dicta as 'God runs through the world like honey through a honeycomb'. Could not Jesus have done as well?

What we must not do is to shrug our shoulders in bafflement and pigeonhole the document. Even supposing it to be tinged with Gnosticism, we still have to ask what it was in Jesus' teaching that encouraged that heresy. It could not have sprung out of nothing. This will be discussed more fully at a later stage.

Another recently discovered source is *The Secret Gospel of Mark*, said to have been taken by him to Alexandria, where he later became the bishop.[9] Sections are quoted by Clement of Alexandria (c.150-c.215 A.D.) in a letter. The most important is the following account of the raising of a young man from the dead, closely similar to John's account of the raising of Lazarus:

And they came to Bethany, and a certain woman, whose brother had died, was there. And coming, she prostrated herself before Jesus and said to him, 'Son of David, have mercy on me'. But the disciples rebuked her. And Jesus, being angered, went off with her into the garden where the tomb was, and straightway a great cry was heard from the tomb. And going near, Jesus rolled away the stone from the door of the tomb. And straightway, going in where the youth was, he stretched forth his hand and raised him, seizing his hand, But the youth, looking upon him, loved him and began to beseech him that he might be with him. And going

18

out of the tomb they came into the house of the youth, for he was rich. And after six days Jesus told him what to do and in the evening the youth came to him, wearing a linen cloth over (his) naked (body). And he remained with him that night, for Jesus taught him the mystery of the kingdom of God. And thence, arising he returned to the other side of Jordan.

The last detail, of Jesus' having the youth come to him naked except for a linen cloth, recalls several passages in *The Gospel of Thomas* enjoining nudity. It accords quite well with what is known of initiation rites among the Gnostic sects of Egypt; and the underlying idea, no doubt, was a symbolic stripping off of everything connected with the present material world. Once more there would seem to have been some doctoring of the original text. The above passage fits in neatly into Mark's present text and raises the question whether Mark wrote another gospel or merely expanded his original one. Clement's words rather imply the latter.

The *Egerton Papyrus*, discovered in 1935 and datable to about 140 A.D., is less valuable. It seems to be a fragment from a non-surviving gospel conflated from the Synoptics and John, but does at least refute the German scholar Baur's theory that John's gospel was written as late as 170 A.D.

No others of what are called the non-canonical gospels, not given the imprimatur of the Church, add anything to our knowledge of Jesus; and, much more surprisingly, the Jewish historian Josephus barely mentions him or Christianity except in a paragraph which seems to have been tampered with.[10] However, he is a very valuable source on the historical background, particularly with regard to the Zealots. He himself was a very colourful figure, who, against his own political judgement, became one of the six regional commanders in the 66 A.D. revolt against Rome. Under his command Jotapata held out against a determined Roman siege for 45 days. When the city fell, he and forty others took refuge in a cave. Josephus was in favour of surrender; but the others found this idea outrageous, preferred death, and threatened his life. Instead, on his proposal, they resolved on a suicide pact. Each was to slay another in an order determined by a drawing of lots, which Josephus held; and, whether by good fortune or by legerdemain, he found himself left at last alone with one other. They agreed not to shed Jewish blood, and Josephus surrendered to the tribune Nicanor, whom he had met previously in Rome. There was still the question of what should become of him in Roman hands. But he succeeded in finding favour with the Roman commander Vespasian by correctly predicting his elevation to the imperial purple, became an imperial protegé, and lived thenceforth in Rome. There he wrote his historical works, *The Jewish War* and *Jewish Antiquities* – a valuable quarry for New Testament scholarship.

The Roman historian Tacitus only confirms that Jesus was indeed executed by order of Pontius Pilate, and reveals that Christians were unpopular and regarded as enemies of society.

THE GOSPEL OF THOMAS

These are the secret sayings which the living Jesus spoke and which Didymos Judas Thomas wrote down.

1. And he said, 'Whoever finds the interpretation of these sayings will not experience death.'

2. Jesus said, 'Let him who seeks continue seeking until he finds. When he finds he will become troubled. When he becomes troubled, he will be astonished, and he will rule over all.'

3. Jesus said, 'If those who lead you say to you, "See, the Kingdom of Heaven is in the sky", then the birds of the sky will precede you. If they say to you, "It is in the sea", then the fish will precede you. Rather, the Kingdom is inside of you. When you come to know yourselves, then you will become known, and you will realise that it is you who are the sons of the living Father. But if you will not know yourselves, you dwell in poverty and it is you who are that poverty.'

4. Jesus said, 'The man old in days will not hesitate to ask a small child seven days old about the place of life, and he will live. For many who are first will become last, and they will become one and the same.'

5. Jesus said, 'Recognise what is in your sight, and that which is hidden from you will become plain to you. For there is nothing hidden which will not become manifest.'

6. His disciples questioned him and said to him, 'Do you want us to fast? How shall we pray? Shall we give alms? What diet shall we observe?'

Jesus said, 'Do not tell lies, and do not do what you hate, for all things are plain in the sight of Heaven. For nothing hidden will not become manifest, and nothing covered will remain without being uncovered.'

7. Jesus said, 'Blessed is the lion which becomes man when consumed by man; and cursed is the man whom the lion consumes.'

8. And he said, 'The man is like a wise fisherman who cast his net into the sea and drew it up from the sea full of small fish. Among them the fisherman found a fine large fish. He threw all the small fish back into the sea and chose the large fish without difficulty. Whoever has ears to hear, let him hear.'

9. Jesus said, 'Now the sower went out, took a handful (of seeds), and scattered them. Some fell on the road; the birds came and gathered them up. Others fell on rock, did not take root in the soil, and did not produce ears. And others fell on thorns; they choked the seed(s) and worms ate them. And others fell on the good soil and produced good fruit: it bore sixty per measure and a hundred and twenty per measure.'

10. Jesus said, 'I have cast fire upon the world, and see, I am guarding it until it blazes.'

11. Jesus said, 'This heaven will pass away, and the one above it will pass away. The dead are not alive, and the living will not die. In the days when you consumed what is dead, you made it what is alive. When you come into the light, what will you do? On the day when you were one you became two. But when you become two, what will you do?'

12. The disciples said to Jesus, 'We know that you will depart from us. Who is to become our leader?' Jesus said to them, 'Wherever you are, you are to go to James the Righteous, for whose sake heaven and earth came into being.'

13. Jesus said to his disciples, 'Compare me to someone and tell me who I am like.'

Simon Peter said to him, 'You are like a righteous angel.'
Matthew said to him, 'You are like a wise philosopher.'

Thomas said to him, 'Master, my mouth is wholly incapable of saying what you are like.'

Jesus said, 'I am not your master. Because you have drunk, you have become intoxicated from the bubbling spring which I have measured out.'

And he took him and withdrew and told him three things. When Thomas returned to his companions, they asked him, 'What did Jesus say to you?' Thomas said to them, 'If I tell you one of the things which he told me, you will pick up stones and throw them at me; a fire will come out of the stones and burn you up.'

14. Jesus said to them, 'If you fast, you will give rise to sins for yourselves; and if you pray, you will be condemned; and if you give alms, you will do harm to your spirits. When you go into any land and walk about in the districts, if they receive you, eat what they will set before you, and heal the sick among them. For what goes into your mouth will not defile you, but that which issues from your mouth – it is that which will defile you.'

15. Jesus said, 'When you see one who was not born of woman, prostrate yourselves on your faces and worship him. That one is your Father.'

16. Jesus said, 'Men think, perhaps, that it is peace which I have come to cast upon the world. They do not know that it is dissension which I have come to cast upon the earth: fire, sword, and war. For there will be five in a house: three will be against two, and two against three, the father against the son, and the son against the father. And they will stand solitary.'

17. Jesus said, 'I shall give you what no eye has seen and what no ear has heard and what no hand has touched and what has never occurred to the human mind.'

18. The disciples said to Jesus, 'Tell us how our end will be.'
Jesus said, 'Have you discovered, then, the beginning, that you

look for the end? For where the beginning is, there the end will be. Blessed is he who will take his place in the beginning: he will know the end and will not experience death.'

19. Jesus said, 'Blessed is he who came into being before he came into being. If you become my disciples and listen to my words, these stones will minister to you. For there are five trees for you in Paradise which remain undisturbed summer and winter and whose leaves do not fall. Whoever becomes acquainted with them will not experience death.'

20. The disciples said to Jesus, 'Tell us what the Kingdom of Heaven is like.'

He said to them, 'It is like a mustard seed, the smallest of all seeds. But when it falls on tilled soil, it produces a great plant and becomes a shelter for the birds of the sky.'

21. Mary said to Jesus, 'Whom are your disciples like?'

He said, 'They are like children who have settled in a field which is not theirs. When the owners of the field come they will say 'Let us have back our field'. They (will) undress in their presence in order to let them have back their field and to give it back to them. Therefore I say to you, if the owner of the house knows that the thief is coming, he will begin his vigil before he comes and will not let him dig through into his house of his domain to carry away his goods. You, then, be on your guard against the world. Arm yourselves with great strength lest the robbers find a way to come to you, for the difficulty which you expect will (surely) materialise. Let there be among you a man of understanding. When the grain ripened, he came quickly with his sickle in his hand and reaped it. Whoever has ears to hear, let him hear.'

22. Jesus saw infants being suckled. He said to his disciples, 'These infants being suckled are like those who enter the Kingdom.'

They said to him, 'Shall we then, as children, enter the Kingdom?'

Jesus said to them, 'When you make the two one, and when you make the inside like the outside and the outside like the inside, and the above like the below, and when you make the male and the female one and the same, so that male be not male nor the female female, and when you fashion eyes in the place of an eye, and a hand in place of a hand, and a foot in place of a foot, and a likeness in place of a likeness, then you will enter (the Kingdom).'

23. Jesus said, 'I shall choose you, one out of a thousand, and two out of ten thousand, and they shall stand as a single one.'

24. His disciples said to him, 'Show us the place where you are, since it is necessary for us to seek it.'

He said to them, 'Whoever has ears, let him hear. There is light within a man of light, and he (or: it) lights up the whole world. If he (or: it) does not shine, he (or: it) is darkness.'

25. Jesus said, 'Love your brother like your soul, guard him like the pupil of your eye.'

26. Jesus said, 'You see the mote in your brother's eye, but you do not see the beam in your own eye. When you cast the beam out of your own eye, then you will see clearly to cast the mote from your brother's eye.'

27. (Jesus said), 'If you do not fast as regards the world, you will not find the Kingdom. If you do not observe the Sabbath as a Sabbath, you will not see the Father.'

28. Jesus said, 'I took my place in the midst of the world, and I appeared to them in flesh. I found them all intoxicated; I found none of them thirsty. And my soul became afflicted for the sons of men, because they are blind in their hearts and do not have sight; for empty they came into the world, and empty they seek to leave the world. But for the moment they are intoxicated. When they shake off their wine, then they will repent.'

29. Jesus said, 'If the flesh came into being because of spirit, it is a wonder. But if spirit came into being because of the body, it

is a wonder of wonders. Indeed, I am amazed at how great this wealth has made its home in this poverty.'

30. Jesus said, 'Where there are three gods, they are gods. Where there are two or one, I am with him.'

31. Jesus said, 'No prophet is accepted in his own village; no physician heals those who know him.'

32. Jesus said, 'A city being built on a high mountain and fortified cannot fall, nor can it be hidden.'

33. Jesus said, 'Preach from your housetops that which you will hear in your ear. For no one lights a lamp and puts it under a bushel, nor does he put it in a hidden place, but rather he sets it on a lampstand so that everyone who enters and leaves will see its light.'

34. Jesus said, 'If a blind man leads a blind man, they will both fall into a pit.'

35. Jesus said, 'It is not possible for anyone to enter the house of a strong man and take it by force unless he binds his hands; then he will (be able to) ransack his house.'

36. Jesus said, 'Do not be concerned from morning until evening and from evening until morning about what you will wear.'

37. His disciples said, 'When will you become revealed to us and when shall we see you?'

Jesus said, 'When you disrobe without being ashamed and take up your garments and place them under your feet like little children and tread on them, then (will you see) the Son of the Living One and you will not be afraid.'

38. Jesus said, 'Many times have you desired to hear these words which I am saying to you, and you have no one else to hear them from. There will be days when you will look for me and will not find me.'

39. Jesus said, 'The Pharisees and the scribes have taken the keys of Knowledge and hidden them. They themselves have not entered, nor have they allowed to enter those who wish

to. You, however, be as wise as serpents and as innocent as doves.'

40. Jesus said, 'A grapevine has been planted outside of the Father, but being unsound, it will be pulled up by its roots and destroyed.'

41. Jesus said, 'Whoever has something in his hand will receive more, and whoever has nothing will be deprived of even the little he has.'

42. Jesus said, 'Become passers-by.'

43. His disciples said to him, 'Who are you, that you should say these things to us?'

(Jesus said to them,) 'You do not realise who I am from what I say to you, but you have become like the Jews, for they (either) love the tree and hate its fruit (or) love the fruit and hate the tree.'

44. Jesus said, 'Whoever blasphemes against the Father will be forgiven, and whoever blasphemes against the Son will be forgiven, but whoever blasphemes against the Holy Spirit will not be forgiven either on earth or in heaven.'

45. Jesus said, 'Grapes are not harvested from thorns, nor are figs gathered from thistles, for they do not produce fruit. A good man brings forth good things from his storehouse; an evil man brings forth evil things from his evil storehouse, which is in his heart, and says evil things. For out of the abundance of the heart he brings forth evil things.'

46. Jesus said, 'Among those born of women, from Adam until John the Baptist, there is no one so superior to John the Baptist that his eyes should not be lowered (before him). Yet I have said, whichever of you comes to be a child will be acquainted with his Kingdom and will become superior to John.'

47. Jesus said, 'It is impossible for a man to mount two horses or to stretch two bows. And it is impossible for a servant to serve two masters; otherwise, he will honour the one and treat the

other contemptuously. No man drinks old wine and immediately desires to drink new wine. And new wine is not put into old wineskins, lest they burst; nor is old wine put into a new wineskin, lest it spoil it. An old patch is not sewn onto a new garment, because a tear would result.'

48. Jesus said, 'If two make peace with each other in this house, they will say to the mountain, "Move away", and it will move away.'

49. Jesus said, 'Blessed are the solitary and elect, for you will find the Kingdom. For you are from it and to it you will return.'

50. Jesus said, 'If they say to you, "Where did you come from?" say to them, "We came from the light, the place where the light came into being on its own accord and established (itself) and became manifest through their image." If they say to you "Is it you?" say, "We are its children, and we are the elect of the Living Father." If they ask you, "What is the sign of your father in you?" say to them, "It is movement and repose."'

51. His disciples said to him, 'When will the repose of the dead come about, and when will the new world come?'

He said to them, 'What you look forward to has already come, but you do not recognise it.'

52. His disciples said to him, 'Twenty-four prophets spoke in Israel, and all of them spoke in you.'

He said to them, 'You have omitted the one living in your presence and have spoken (only) of the dead.'

53. His disciples said to him, 'Is circumcision beneficial or not?'

He said to them, 'If it were beneficial, their father would beget them already circumcised from their mother. Rather, the true circumcision in spirit has become completely profitable.'

54. Jesus said, 'Blessed are the poor, for yours is the Kingdom of Heaven.'

55. Jesus said, 'Whoever does not hate his father and his mother cannot become a disciple to me. And whoever does not

hate his brothers and sisters and take up his cross in my way will not be worthy of me.'

56. Jesus said, 'Whoever has come to understand the world has found (only) a corpse, and whoever has found a corpse is superior to the world.'

57. Jesus said, 'The Kingdom of the Father is like a man who had (good) seed. His enemy came by night and sowed weeds among the good seed. The man did not allow them to pull up the weeds; he said to them, "I am afraid that you will go intending to pull up the weeds and pull up the wheat along with them." For on the day of the harvest the weeds will be plainly visible, and they will be pulled up and burned.'

58. Jesus said, 'Blessed is the man who has suffered and found life.'

59. Jesus said, 'Take heed of the Living One while you are alive, lest you die and seek to see him and be unable to do so.'

60. (They saw) a Samaritan carrying a lamb on his way to Judaea. He said to his disciples, '(Why does) that man (carry) the lamb around?'

They said to him, 'So that he may kill it and eat it.'

He said to them, 'While it is alive, he will not eat it, but only when he has killed it and it has become a corpse.'

They said to him, 'He cannot do otherwise.'

He said to them, 'You too, look for a place for yourselves within Repose, lest you become a corpse and be eaten.'

61. Jesus said, 'Two will rest on a bed: the one will die, and the other will live.'

Salome said, 'Who are you, man, that you, as though from the One, (or: (whose son)), that you have come up on my couch and eaten from my table?'

Jesus said to her, 'I am He who exists from the Undivided. I was given some of the things of my Father.'

(Salome said,) 'I am your disciple.'

(Jesus said to her) 'Therefore I say, if he is (undivided), he will be filled with light, but if he is divided he will be filled with darkness.'

62. Jesus said, 'It is to those (who are worthy of my) mysteries that I tell my mysteries. Do not let your left hand know what your right hand is doing.'

63. Jesus said, 'There was a rich man who had much money. He said, "I shall put my money to use so that I may sow, reap, plant, and fill my storehouse with produce, with the result that I shall lack nothing." Such were his intentions, but that same night he died. Let him who has ears hear.'

64. See page 62.

65. He said, 'There was a man who owned a vineyard. He leased it to tenant farmers so that they might work it and he might collect the produce from them. He sent his servant so that the tenants might give him the produce of the vineyard. They seized his servant and beat him, all but killing him. The servant went back and told his master. The master said, "Perhaps (they) did not recognise (him)." He sent another servant. The tenants beat this one as well. Then the owner sent his son and said, "Perhaps they will show respect to my son." Because the tenants knew that it was he who was heir to the vineyard, they seized him and killed him. Let him who has ears hear.'

66. Jesus said, 'Show me the stone which the builders have rejected. That one is the cornerstone.'

67. Jesus said, 'Whoever believes that the All itself is deficient is (himself) completely deficient.'

68. Jesus said, 'Blessed are you when you are hated and persecuted. Wherever you have been persecuted they will find no place.'

69. Jesus said, 'Blessed are they who have been persecuted within themselves. It is they who have truly come to know the Father. Blessed are the hungry, for the belly of him who desires will be filled.'

70. Jesus said, 'That which you have will save you if you bring

it forth from yourselves. That which you do not have within you will kill you if you do not have it within you.'

71. Jesus said, 'I shall destroy (this) house and no one will be able to rebuild it.'

72. (A man said) to him, 'Tell my brothers to divide my father's possessions with me.'

He said to him, 'O man, who has made me a divider?' He turned to his disciples and said to them, 'I am not a divider, am I?'

73. Jesus said, 'The harvest is great, but the labourers are few. Beseech the Lord, therefore, to send out labourers to the harvest.'

74. He said, 'O Lord, there are many around the drinking-trough, but there is none in the cistern.'

75. Jesus said, 'Many are standing at the door, but it is the solitary who will enter the bridal chamber.'

76. Jesus said, 'The Kingdom of the Father is like a merchant who had a consignment of merchandise and who discovered a pearl. That merchant was shrewd. He sold the merchandise and bought the pearl alone for himself. You too, seek his unfailing and enduring treasure where no moth comes near to devour and no worm destroys.'

77. Jesus said, 'It is I who am the light which is above them all. It is I who am the All. From me did the All come forth, and unto me did the All extend. Split a piece of wood, and I am there. Lift up the stone and you will find me there.'

78. Jesus said, 'Why have you come out into the desert? To see a reed shaken by the wind? And to see a man clothed in fine garments like your kings and your great men? Upon them are the (fine) garments, and they are unable to discern the truth.'

79. A woman from the crowd said unto him, 'Blessed are the womb which bore you and the breasts which nourished you.'

He said to her, 'Blessed are those who have heard the word of the Father and have kept it. For there will be days when you will say, "Blessed are the womb which has not conceived and the breasts which have not given milk".'

80. Jesus said, 'He who has recognised the world has found the body, but he who has found the body is superior to the world.'

81. Jesus said, 'Let him who has grown rich be king, and let him who possesses power renounce it.'

82. Jesus said, 'He who is near me is near the fire, and he who is far from me is far from the Kingdom.'

83. Jesus said, 'The images are manifest to man, but the light in them remains concealed in the image of the light of the Father. He will become manifest, but his image will remain concealed by his light.'

84. Jesus said, 'When you see your likeness, you rejoice. But when you see your images which came into being before you, and which neither die nor become manifest, how much you will have to bear!'

85. Jesus said, 'Adam came into being from a great power and a great wealth, but he did not become worthy of you. For had he been worthy, (he would) not (have experienced) death.'

86. Jesus said, '(The foxes have their holes) and the birds have (their) nests, but the Son of Man has no place to lay his head and rest.'

87. Jesus said, 'Wretched is the body that is dependent upon a body, and wretched is the soul that is dependent upon these two.'

88. Jesus said, 'The angels and the prophets will come to you and give to you those things you (already) have. And you too, give them those things which you have, and say to yourselves, "When will they come and take what is theirs?".'

89. Jesus said, 'Why do you wash the outside of the cup? Do you not realise that he who made the inside is the same one who made the outside?'

90. Jesus said, 'Come unto me, for my yoke is easy and my lordship is mild, and you will find repose for yourselves.'

91. They said to him, 'Tell us who you are so that we may believe in you.'

He said to them, 'You read the face of the sky and of the earth, but you have not recognised the one who (or: that which) is before you, and you do not know how to read this moment.'

92. Jesus said, 'Seek and you will find. Yet, what you asked me about in former times and which I did not tell you then, now I do desire to tell, but you do not enquire after it.'

93. (Jesus said), 'Do not give what is holy to dogs, lest they throw them on the dung heap. Do not throw the pearls to swine, lest they grind it (to bits).'

94. Jesus said, 'He who seeks will find, and (he who knocks) will be let in.'

95. (Jesus said), 'If you have money, do not lend it at interest, but give it to one from whom you will not get it back.'

96. Jesus (said), 'The Kingdom of the Father is like a certain woman. She took a little leaven, (concealed) it in some dough, and made it into large loaves. Let him who has ears hear.'

97. Jesus said, 'The Kingdom of the (Father) is like a certain woman who was carrying a jar full of meal. While she was walking (on) a road, still some distance from home the handle of the jar broke and the meal emptied out behind her on the road. She did not realise it; she had noticed no accident. When she reached her house, she set the jar down and found it empty.'

98. Jesus said, 'The Kingdom of the Father is like a certain man who wanted to kill a powerful man. In his own house he drew his sword and stuck it into the wall in order to find out whether his hand could carry through. Then he slew the powerful man.'

99. The disciples said to him, 'Your brothers and your mother are standing outside.'

He said to them, 'Those here who do the will of My Father are my brothers and my mother. It is they who will enter the Kingdom of My Father.'

100. They showed Jesus a gold coin and said to him, 'Caesar's men demand taxes from us.'

He said to them, 'Give Caesar what belongs to Caesar, give God what belongs to God, and give me what is mine.'

101. (Jesus said), 'Whoever does not hate his father and his mother as I do cannot become a disciple to me. And whoever does (not) love his father and his mother as I do cannot become a (disciple) to me. For my mother (gave me falsehood), but (my) true (mother) gave me life.'

102. Jesus said, 'Woe to the Pharisees, for they are like a dog sleeping in the manger of oxen, for neither does he eat nor does he let the oxen eat.'

103. Jesus said, 'Fortunate is the man who knows where the brigands will enter, so that he may get up, muster his domain, and arm himself before they invade.'

104. They said (to Jesus), 'Come, let us pray today and let us fast.'

Jesus said, 'What is the sin that I have committed, or wherein have I been defeated? But when the bridegroom leaves the bridal chamber, then let them fast and pray.'

105. Jesus said, 'He who knows the father and mother will be called the son of a harlot.'

106. Jesus said, 'When you make the two one, you will become the sons of man, and when you say, "Mountain, move away," it will move away.'

107. Jesus said, 'The kingdom is like a shepherd who had a hundred sheep. One of them, the largest, went astray. He left the ninety-nine and looked for that one until he found it. When he had found it, he said to the sheep, "I care for you more than the ninety-nine".'

108. Jesus said, 'He who will drink from my mouth will become like me. I myself shall become he, and things that are hidden will be revealed to him.'

109. Jesus said, 'The Kingdom is like a man who had a

(hidden) treasure in his field without knowing it. And (after) he died, he left it to his son. The son did not know (about the treasure). He inherited the field and sold (it). And the one who bought it went ploughing and found the treasure. He began to lend money at interest to whomever he wished.'

110. Jesus said, 'Whoever finds the world and becomes rich, let him renounce the world.'

111. Jesus said, 'The heavens and the earth will be rolled up in your presence. And the one who lives from the Living One will not see death.' Does not Jesus say, 'Whoever finds himself is superior to the world'?

112. Jesus said, 'Woe to the flesh that depends upon the soul; woe to the soul that depends upon the flesh.'

113. His disciples said to him, 'When will the Kingdom come?'

(Jesus said,) 'It will not come by waiting for it. It will not be a matter of saying "Here it is or There it is." Rather, the Kingdom of the Father is spread out upon the earth, and men do not see it.'

114. Simon Peter said to them, 'Let Mary leave us, for women are not worthy of Life.'

Jesus said, 'I myself shall lead her in order to make her male, so that she too may become a living spirit resembling you males. For every woman who will make herself male will enter the Kingdom of Heaven.'

(Translation: Thomas O. Lambdin, from J.M. Robinson, *The Nag Hammadi Library*, New York, Harper & Row, 3rd revised edition, 1989)

MISSION AND MESSIAHSHIP

There were no registry offices and school records in the ancient world. So, even in the case of famous persons, no notice was taken of their existence until they had achieved some status within the community. Little is generally known of their early years except perhaps for some striking anecdote, such as that about the Athenian statesman Alcibiades and his unfair play methods. (He resorted to biting.)

Similarly we know nothing reliable about Jesus' toddler years. But Luke (2.41-52) relates a significant story of an incident when he was twelve. It was the practice of his parents to go to Jerusalem every year for the Passover festival; and in the year concerned they made the pilgrimage as usual. When the festival was over, they started off home with their friends and neighbours, assuming that the boy was with the party, and only discovered that he was not when the party made its first stop. Then, returning in haste, they found him still in the temple, sitting among the teachers and listening to their theological discussions. This is just the kind of tale that would be often repeated in family circles and stay long in neighbourhood memory. It indicates a child of extraordinary promise and of religious temperament.[1]

The next twenty odd years are a complete blank. Perhaps Jesus had to act as the family breadwinner; for according to tradition Joseph was already an old man when he was born, and life was short in those times. Contrary to a modern hymn, however, he would not have worked at the plane and the lathe, since the latter tool was not then invented. He may not even have been a carpenter at all, since the Aramaic word for *tecton* could equally well mean 'scholar'. But how he earned his living is not important.

Again according to Luke, Jesus' mission began when he was about thirty years old after his baptism by John the Baptist, his near relative. John had appeared out of the desert, clothed like a prophet of old in camel's hair, with a leathern girdle about his loins, and feeding only on locusts and wild honey. (A modern translation changes 'locusts' to 'carobs' (a leguminous plant) – perhaps unnecessarily; for locusts are offered for food in Burma.) He called people to be baptised as a sign of their repentance and to seek forgiveness of their sins; and they flocked to him from all directions.

Jesus came along with others, and enjoyed what would now be called a religious experience[2], hearing a voice declare: 'You are my beloved son, in whom I am well pleased.' It is plain from the original Greek that the voice need not have been audible to bystanders.

Surprisingly, to a Hebrew the words would not have meant son of God in the literal sense. They indicated merely special divine favour and protection; and this is clearly the meaning in Psalm 2, where God is represented as saying to the king of Israel 'Thou art my son; this day have I begotten thee.' Later, after the fall of the Hebrew monarchy, it was quite natural for the phrase 'Son of God' to be used of the promised Messiah, who was to restore dominion to Israel. Thus in Jesus' trial before the Sanhedrin the High Priest asks him 'Are you the Messiah, the Son of God?' (Matt. 26.64), the *christos* of the Greek being a translation of the Hebrew title. This is the only certain instance of this linkage; but it is sufficient.

Jesus must have had some previous inklings of his vocation; or he would not have walked over 70 miles from Nazareth. But he was not necessarily prepared for so major a summons, and he would naturally have felt a need for undisturbed, even solitary, reflection. So we read that he 'was led up of the Spirit into the wilderness to be tempted of the devil. And when he had fasted forty days and forty nights he was afterward anhungered.'

The forty days are, of course, merely a conventional round figure for a long period; and the fasting need not have been absolute – although recent examples of hunger-strikers show how long mental and physical vigour can be maintained in the absence of solid nourishment. For the devil we may legitimately read Jesus' own inner musings and doubts. Had the voice been merely a matter of imagination? ('*If* you are the Son of God . . .') Or precisely to what kind of mission was he being summoned? And how was he to go about his task? It is important that we should interpret the picturesque Bible account of these temptations and of Jesus' reaction to them correctly; for only so will we have the right guidelines for piecing together a true account of his later career from the Bible narrative. Mark (or his epitomizer) was strangely imperceptive in giving us only a one-line summary. For convenience of reference I quote Matthew's account in the familiar *Authorised Version*:

> And when the tempter came to him, he said, If thou be the Son of God, command that these stones be made bread. But he answered and said, It is written, Man shall not live by bread alone, but by every word that proceedeth out of the mouth of God.
>
> Then the devil taketh him up into the holy city, and setteth him on a pinnacle of the temple, and saith unto him, If thou be the Son of God, cast thyself down: for it is written, He shall give his angels charge concerning thee: and in their hands they shall bear thee up . . . Jesus said unto him, It is written again, Thou shalt not tempt the Lord thy God.
> Again, the devil taketh him up into an exceeding high mountain, and sheweth him all the kingdoms of the world, and the glory of them; and saith unto him, All these things will I give thee, if thou wilt fall down and worship me. Then saith Jesus unto him, Get

thee hence, Satan: for it is written, Thou shalt worship the Lord thy God, and him only shalt thou serve. (Matt. 4.1-10)

No modern rationalist, but the third century scholar Origen considered these transactions not a record of external occurrences, but rather Jesus's inward reflections, related afterwards to his followers in parable form. There is in fact no mountain from which all the kingdoms of the world can be seen – even of the Roman world; and the flight to the topmost pinnacle of the temple was also merely a flight of fancy. The arguments by quotation from the Scriptures are quite in the Jewish tradition.

Our interpretation depends on whether we assume Jesus to have been already conscious of an ability to draw on divine powers at will and sure of divine protection. In that case the temptations related solely to the methods of ministry he should adopt. This is the traditional view. But note that they all begin with the word 'if'. This implies a doubt in his mind.

The first temptation was, then, a test of faith, inviting him to resolve this doubt by a simple experiment. This would both relieve his hunger and provide the desired certainty. It would, though, imply a doubting of what he believed was God's own voice. His rejection of the idea indicates a decision to trust in his vision and put his hand to the work that it suggested.

The difficulty is that Jesus' quotation from Deuteronomy (8.3) does not seem to fit the occasion. It recalls the time when the Israelites began questioning the wisdom of their exodus from Egypt and had their doubts removed by the gift of manna. Accordingly Bishop Gore[3] relates it to Jesus' later injunction to 'seek first the Kingdom of God and his righteousness', when other, material, needs would be provided for. But the main point of the reference was the Israelites' lack of faith and trust in God's guidance as revealed through Moses; and the issue was whether Jesus would comply with God's command, given this time directly and not at second hand. It was not an invitation to solve the world's economic problems with a sweep of the divine wand.

If the first temptation might be taken as a call to Jesus to see whether he really had divine *powers*, the second might be regarded as a challenge to establish whether he was indeed under divine *protection*. A modern equivalent would be to dare someone to attempt a hazardous climb of a rock face without companions or previous training. But, since he had already resolved to rely on God's guidance, this second experiment would have been superfluous. *The New English Bible* translates Deuteronomy 6.16 here as 'You must not challenge the Lord your God,' i.e. you must not presume too far upon his well-known qualities of love and protectiveness. The question was whether Jesus should attempt to establish his authority with some spectacular display or miracle. He spurned the invitation, and it is vital to remember this when dealing with the record of his future career.

The last temptation has been explained by reference to the attempts of some political prelates to advance the cause of Christianity by diplomatic manoeuvring and intrigues. But this does not fit the circumstances of the first century of our era and Jesus' situation in these. In that context using the way of the world could only have been to put himself forward as a Warrior Messiah and seek both to liberate his own people and to gain further wide empire.

The project was less chimerical than might appear. The frontier force that protected the Roman empire was relatively small – some 170,000 legionaries and a similar number of auxiliaries, or not much more than 300,000 men in all. Compared with the masses deployed in the Second World War the numbers are derisory and were in fact barely adequate in the first centuries A.D. The Romans were banking on the chance that there would not be threats on two sectors of the frontiers at the same time. The Jews might, therefore, have had reasonable prospects of success if they could secure the support of strong allies.

A strong ally was near at hand in the form of the Parthian empire. Its mounted archers were adept at a war of movement, and they had destroyed three Roman legions in 53 B.C.; and they were to force the capitulation of another Roman force at Rhandeia in 63 A.D. But when the Jews did finally revolt in improvised fashion in 66 A.D., Parthia had already made its peace with Rome. In 29 A.D. Parthia still had ambitions to control Armenia. So, under a dynamic leader the Jews might have anticipated the successes of Mohammed.

This was the kind of Messiah traditionally expected by the Jewish people; and it was a prospect to stir the heart of any patriotic Jew. But such a role was manifestly inconsistent with Jesus' teaching and character. His own conception of the Messiah was to be far different, although he had, perhaps, still to formulate it with precision. What was already clear to him was that his status must be kept secret so as not to arouse the wrong expectations. There was the same objection to a public declaration as to an attempt to gain allegiance through a display of conspicuous miracles. The public would be led to accept his teaching, not on its merits, but on the grounds of its author's prestige. So he laid no public claim to the title.

His disciples, however, soon guessed the truth. Andrew (John 1.20) is said to have recruited Peter with the words 'We have found the Messiah'; and Philip approached Nathanael in much the same way. (Here Nathanael's 'Can anything good come out of Nazareth?' is a very authentic touch.) The incident reported in Mark 8.28ff also probably occurred in the early days. Questioned by Jesus as to the disciples' own view of his identity, Peter replies: 'You are the Messiah.' Jesus acknowledges the identification, but immediately gives instructions that the fact is not to be revealed. Soon afterwards in Mark's narrative Jesus makes a triumphal entry into Jerusalem in a manner that proclaims to the world that he is indeed the promised Messiah; and one wonders what was the point of a concealment that was so soon to be cancelled. Mark did not, warns Papias (p. 12 above), record events in their true order; and this seems to be an obvious instance.[4]

Nor should too much be made of Jesus' references to himself as 'the Son of Man.' This appears at first sight as a major claim indeed, implying the doctrine of the Incarnation. But Prof. Vermes[5] has shown conclusively that this Aramaic phrase (*bar nasha*) was used in ordinary discourse as the equivalent of 'I' or me – much as the English 'one'. Its frequent use by Jesus might have been an individual trick of speech similar to my own sixth-form master's over-addiction to 'one' – a mannerism which afforded rich opportunities for dormitory humour. The difference is that the Aramaic *bar nasha* tended to be used when unpleasant possibilities were in view, whereas the English 'one' implies that the hearer will agree with the view expressed.

It is possible that Jesus used the phrase with calculated ambiguity, with one meaning for his immediate entourage and another for the general public. Most instances in the Synoptic Gospels refer to his missionary status; but in John's Gospel it often has a definitely christological reference, e.g. John 6.28: 'This food (of eternal life) the Son of Man will give you.' J.A.T. Robinson[6] argued that at least the basis of this work came from the apostle John; and, if so, this would mean that for the disciples the combination of words had a special significance. However, for the moment the important point is that the ordinary bystander would have seen Jesus' use of the expression as at most a personal idiosyncracy, and not a theological title.

The general shape of his mission once decided, Jesus' next task would have been to gain an audience and followers; and the obvious means to this would have been to attach himself as an assistant to John the Baptist. So the Fourth Gospel is probably right in suggesting a joint mission, with Jesus taking over on John's imprisonment by Herod.

THE MIRACLES

Jesus seems, then, to have resolved not to startle men into faith by a display of miraculous powers. It comes as a surprise, therefore, that in his second chapter Mark goes on to relate the first of a series of exorcisms and miraculous feats of healing by him. In some instances Jesus binds the recovered patient to secrecy about his good fortune (mostly unsuccessfully), but he is also reported to have performed cures publicly in a synagogue and before lawyers and Pharisees. Jesus, if anyone, would have been moved to compassion by the sight of human suffering; and the exercise of powers of healing was quite different in moral quality from a stuntlike leap from an eminence. But, if he wished to keep his Messiahship secret, this was no way to do so. And the modern reader must feel surprised that such curative feats did not make more impression on the religious authorities. Why did they not see them as visible proof that Jesus' mission had divine sanction?

The explanation, to be found in Prof. Vermes' *Jesus the Jew*[1], is also surprising. They had seen something of the kind before.

As compared with Greek medicine, the Jewish was primitive and almost non-existent. The Greeks had long since advanced to the practice of surgery – 'cutting and burning' in Plato's phrase; but the Jews had had no Hippocrates, with his careful analysis of symptoms. All ailments, both mental and physical, were ascribed to the malign action of demons in the service of Satan.

In cases of mental derangement this was understandable, as

readers of Freud and Breuer's *Studies in Hysteria* will discover. In it Breuer relates that the patient Anna O. would complain of having two selves, a real one and an evil one which compelled her to behave badly; and Breuer himself writes (p. 101): 'It is hard to avoid expressing the situation by saying that the patient was split into two personalities of which one was mentally normal and the other insane.' Later (p. 331f.) he develops the theme more fully:

> The splitting of the mind is the consummation of hysteria . . . One part of the patient's mind is in the hypnoid state . . . and is always prepared whenever there is a lapse in waking thought to assume control over the whole person . . . The split off mind is the devil with which the unsophisticated observation of earlier superstitious times believed that these patients were possessed. It is true that a spirit alien to the patient's waking consciousness holds sway within him; but the spirit is in fact not an alien one, but a part of his own.

The assumption of demonic possession was, therefore, a natural one, and rebukes to the evil spirits as much a recognised part of medical routine as the psychiatrist's couch or the doctor's stethoscope today. The sick man's relatives and friends would have expected Jesus to proceed in that way. Otherwise they might not have regarded him as a genuine doctor! In addition, Jewish exorcists attempted mastery of the demons through arcane formulae and incantations. Prof. Vermes quotes a description of an exorcism by a certain Eleazar:

> He put to the nose of the possessed man a ring which had under its seal one of the roots prescribed by Solomon, and then, as the man smelled it, drew out the demon through his nostrils, and, when the man at once fell down, adjured the demon never to come back into him, speaking Solomon's name and reciting the incantations which he had composed.[2]

Investigations into medical roots were a leading activity of the

Essenes, and Prof. Vermes believes that they were popularly known as The Healers. If so, they would be the people Jesus had in mind when, charged with casting out devils in the name of Beelzebub, he asked 'In whose name do your own people cast them out?'

There are also resemblances between Jesus and the Hasidim. These were holy men who were believed to have supernatural powers due to their immediate relation to God and who, like Jesus, offended the Pharisees by their commonsense attitude to Sabbath observance. One of them, Hanina ben Dosa, is credited with the power to heal from a distance, in the same way that Jesus is said to have healed the centurion's servant. The famous Gamaliel's (Acts 5) son was suffering from a mortal fever, and the father despatched two of his pupils to Hanina for aid. Hanina is related merely to have retired to an upper room and prayed, and then told the youths, 'Go home; for the fever has left him.' Gamaliel later confirmed that the boy had recovered at that very hour.[3]

Another New Testament scholar, N. Perrin[4], points out that there are many examples of exorcism in the Rabbinic tradition, with success either ascribed to prayer or regarded as a reward for some meritorious act. But Jesus' attribution of his cures to the patient's faith is a feature peculiar to himself. Perrin infers that this must be an authentic detail and goes on to note that Jesus was counted as a miracle worker and an exorcist in ancient Jewish texts. The tradition of his healing ministry must accordingly be valid, even though there can be no certainty about all the details of any single miracle story as it now stands.

One suspect detail in Jesus' exorcism cases is the way in which the persons with hysteric symptoms are made to shout out at him as the Son of God. Satan addresses him in the same way in the Temptation story. An age which believed in demonic possession naturally believed that the devils concerned would recognise the Messiah, and this is probably an instance of corroborative colouring added in the days of the early Church when belief in Jesus' divinity had become part of the Creed. It is probably the work, not of Mark himself, but of a later editor.

Another instance of embellishment in accordance with the ideas of the first century A.D. is the reported transfer of the devils into the Gadarene swine. The exorcism by Eleazar referred to above provides a parallel.

> Eleazar placed a cup or foot-basin full of water a little way off and commanded the demon, as it went out of the man, to overturn it and make known to the spectators that it had left the man.[5]

Discounting such accretions to the original narrative, the modern reader may be prepared to accept the possibility of the treatment of mental derangement by means of exorcism and yet feel profoundly sceptical about Jesus' miraculous cures where physical symptoms were concerned. Hysteric symptoms could well respond to psychological treatment. But what are we to make nowadays of the alleged instantaneous healing of the man with a withered arm (Matt. 12.8) and of the paralytic (Matt. 9.6)?

Once more the case of Anna O. is illuminating. In addition to her dual personality problem she was also suffering from an eye squint, stammering, a tightening up of her neck muscles, and paralysis of an arm, only the fingers of which retained to some extent the power of movement. The development of these complaints was finally traced to a painful and traumatic experience while nursing her sick and dying father. Continued lack of sleep had reduced her vitality, so that she was at the time in a drowsy, hypnoid state; and she could no more recall the event when conscious than we often can recall the details of a dream. Her physician had to draw it out from her under hypnosis, and this 'talking cure' finally removed the symptoms.

Another suggestive case is that of a nineteen-year-old girl

who developed a partial paralysis of the legs. Freud discovered this to have been occasioned by the breaking off of her engagement with a fiancé, who was found on closer acquaintance to have a number of undesirable character traits. Once more the physical symptoms were found to be hysteric in character and were dissipated by psychiatric treatment. A similar explanation, in emotional disturbance, may be given for the way in which Christian saints, like St Paul and St Teresa of Avila, developed the stigmata of Jesus' crucifixion; and, if these instances are regarded as too distant and legendary, a more recent case, of a nun, was reported on Radio 4 on 18th April 1993.

Two points are to be noted: (1) the way in which psychic affects can produce somatic and physical symptoms; and (2) the therapeutic power of confiding troubles to someone sympathetic and understanding. Breuer notes with approval the Roman Catholic practice of confession and concludes: 'Telling things is a relief; it discharges tension, even when the person to whom they are told is not a priest, and even when no absolution follows.'[6]

A difference between the modern cases and that of the Gospel paralytic is that he could well remember his sins, and is not recorded as having divulged them. It does not follow that he did not. Scripture may well give us only an abbreviated account; and, if this guess is correct and his symptoms were indeed hysterical, the story becomes easy to accept.

The most difficult of Jesus' cases to explain are those of leprosy. They were probably not instances of leprosy in its modern form. This is a type of elephantiasis and is not curable. The Biblical complaint clearly was so, since those who had recovered from it were required to show themselves to the priests for confirmation of their cured state (Leviticus 13). The confusion arose from the Septuagint's translation of the Hebrew word by *lepra*, an omnibus term which covered such things as ringworm, eczema and even mildew.[7] The possibility of a wrong diagnosis will be familiar to readers of Sherlock Holmes' case of *The Blanched Soldier*. Skin complaints are very commonly of nervous origin; and the really miraculous feature of Jesus' cures of 'lepers' is not the fact of them, but their instantaneity.

How sight could be restored to the blind is harder to divine; but in the case of the man born sightless (Mark 8. 22-26) there is perhaps confirmation of the factual occurrence of the miracle. A G.C.S.E. physics textbook notes that the image on our retinas is inverted and that our brains learn to interpret this correctly — just as a dinghy helmsman must learn to use reverse tiller when sailing backwards or a car mechanic to make use of a mirror when working on certain inaccessible parts of the engine. If so, 'I see men as trees, walking' would be a very accurate description of the image presented to the newly sighted. But perhaps we should beware of building too much upon a passage in a school primer. A thoughtful creator might have offset the inversity of the retina image by means of the 'wiring' from the ganglion cells to the brain.

When healing, not exorcism, was required, Jesus worked generally through laying his hands upon the patient, but in the case of the blind man from Bethsaida he also spat into his eyes, and in that of the deaf-mute put his fingers into the man's ears, touched his tongue with saliva, and gave the command 'Be opened.' We may imagine that besides laying on his hands he also prayed, perhaps with a rapt expression; and that this was what provoked his relatives to seek to take hold of him declaring that he was out of his mind (Matt. 3.21). As Prof. Vermes remarks, 'the scandalous incongruity of this statement is the best guarantee of its authenticity'.

Before writing his book, Prof. Vermes asked a psychiatrist whether most of the ailments remedied by Jesus could be recognised as hysterical. In reply the latter gave a qualified 'Yes', but asked what was the state of the patients six months after discharge.[8] Relapse after faith-healing can be even more swift.

When still a young boy I overheard my parents discussing with friends the visit of a certain Pastor Jeffries to Sunderland. He hired the Victoria Hall and, after a revivalist service of hymns and prayers, invited members of the audience to come up onto the stage for treatment of their complaints. Among those accepting the offer was a man on crutches. The pastor put his hands upon the man's head with a fixed stare and expression upon his face, and then, in a commanding voice, ordered him to throw away his crutches and walk off. The man obeyed and managed to walk home, but collapsed inside the doorway and ended up in a far more serious state than his original one.

I have unfortunately been unable to gain confirmation of this account from the files of *The Sunderland Echo*, despite a careful search by the library staff; but the facts are vouched for by Mr C.E. Bayles, who also lived in Sunderland at the time and was the subject of a successful faith-healing after four years of ordinary medical treatment had failed.[9] The cases sharply illustrate the two faces of faith-healing – the genuine and that of the charlatan.

In all, twelve instances of healing by Jesus are reported in some detail; but Mark represents them as being only a selection from a much greater number. Was that indeed the case? The results of form-criticism raise a doubt. According to this, only the fuller case-histories would come from the apostles' preaching, and the linking narrative would be the work of the evangelist. At the risk of blasphemy we might find a parallel in Tacitus' account of treason trials in the principate of the emperor Tiberius. By a number of rhetorical generalisations such as 'Neither the professional accusers nor Tiberius ever wearied', he contrives to leave in the reader's mind a picture of a reign of terror; but this impression is not supported by a study of the actual trials before the Senate.[10] We have to reflect that Mark is out to portray Jesus as at least semi-divine, and that the main emphasis of his Gospel is upon the aspect of Jesus as a miracle-worker. His work contains accounts of only four parables (three in Chapter 4); and none of these is concerned with the *content* of Jesus' teaching. For his moral and ethical message we have to turn to Matthew and Luke. A fair conclusion is that Jesus did indeed perform miracles of healing, but that Mark exaggerates their number.

Other instances of miracles in the Synoptic Gospels are few, and one readily explicable. This is the calming of the storm on the Sea of Galilee (Mark 4. 39–41). This is a stretch of water peculiarly liable to squalls, which die away as suddenly as they have arisen. The chains of mountains to the east and west, with snow-capped Mount Hermon to the north, form a natural wind-tunnel like the venturi in a solenoid carburettor, intensifying the air flow. In such gusty conditions in an open boat there is nothing so dangerous as panic reactions among some members of the crew. Jesus' order to calm down may well have been directed to one of the disciples. For gusts are commonly followed by 'anti-gusts', so that precipitate over-reaction is highly dangerous.

The Feeding of the Five Thousand, to be found in all four Gospels, (Mark 6.35-44; Matt. 14.15-21; Luke 9.12-17 and John 6.1-13), is not so easily disposed of. John's 'Where are we to buy bread to feed these people?' is reminiscent of Moses' words in Numbers 11.23 ('Where am I to find meat to give them all?') and suggests that Jesus is the new Moses, who will give his people divine food. And the twelve baskets of leftovers recall the similar outcome of the time when Elisha relieved a famine with a mere twenty barley loaves and fresh ripe ears of corn (2 Kings 4.42-44). But we cannot conclude from these parallels that the tale is a fiction devised to make a theological point in symbolic form. That is quite in the manner of John, but quite foreign to the literal, down-to-earth manner of the Synoptics.[11]

A literal acceptance of the account is attended with even greater difficulties. The miraculous feeding of the multitude would have been at odds with Jesus' chosen strategy for his mission. It would have been a bid to gain credence by means he had deliberately forsworn. And it would have revealed the Messiahship which he had enjoined his followers to keep secret. This last objection applies also to the conjecture that the meal was not a substantial repast but a merely symbolic one, after the manner of a Church eucharist – a Messianic Banquet. The only occasion when Jesus could have promoted such a ritual was in the last week before his triumphal entry into Jerusalem.

The most desperate and least convincing of all the explanations offered is the rationalistic one. This is that Jesus took advantage of an offer of the boy with five barley loaves and two small fishes to shame the crowd into sharing the packed lunches the more prudent had brought with them. This accounts neatly for the mound of leftovers; but it is too much like a German scholar's conjecture to explain away the story of Jesus' walking upon the water (Matt. 14.22-43) – that he was in fact paddling upon a sandbank! Stories of miracles are not generated so easily. If authentic, the incident of Jesus' walking on the water is more likely to have been a post-resurrection appearance. Significant too is Matthew's detail that Peter got out from the boat and managed only a few steps before sinking – a visual analogy of the gap in spirituality between Jesus and his chief lieutenant.

A symbolic intent may also be detected in the account of Jesus' exorcism of the daughter of the Syrophoenician woman (Mark 7.24-30; Matt. 15.21-28.). In answer to her plea for aid, Jesus at first makes as if to reject her: 'Let the children be satisfied first; it is not fair to take the children's bread and throw it to the dogs.' But the woman persists. 'Sir', she answers, 'even the dogs under the table eat the children's scraps.' At this Jesus relents, telling her to go home content, since her daughter is healed. Some writers have seized on Jesus' first words to argue that he never intended any mission to the Gentiles. But, if so, why was he in the foreign city of Tyre? And in fact the woman did gain her request. The tendency of the tale is quite the opposite.[12]

Coincidentally, both in this case and in that of the centurion's servant (Matt. 8.5-10), the cure is represented as being effected from a distance, and in each case for the benefit of Gentiles; and in each case too, emphasis is laid upon the healing power of faith. Either Jesus did not confine his mission to the Jews or these stories are two early-Church inventions to justify its wider propagation of the Gospel.

All the instances of miracles dealt with so far come from the Synoptic Gospels. Most of those reported by John have symbolic overtones; and the author has been careful to leave us clues – in the clearly inappropriate words he puts in the mouths of the spiritually unenlightened. The most obvious example comes in Jesus' encounter with a Samaritan woman at Jacob's Well (John 4.15). Jesus tells her that whoever drinks the water (of life) which he can give will never feel thirst again. She jumps at the offer, declaring it will save her a laborious daily journey. Nicodemus also fails to detect Jesus' metaphor (3.4). Told that to enter the Kingdom of God a man must have a rebirth, he asks rhetorically how he can re-enter his mother's womb. The Jews exhibit a similar lack of perception regarding the discourse that follows the miracle of the loaves and fishes. 'I am the bread of life,' Jesus declares. 'Moreover, the bread which I will give is my own flesh; I give it for the life of the world.' 'How can this man give us his flesh to eat?' exclaim the Jews (6.54). All these passages warn the reader that accounts of miracles in John's Gospel are not merely chronicles of marvels that happened long ago. When reading them we have to be alert for metaphor and allegory.

This is particularly true of Jesus' turning of water into wine (2.1-11). Modern readers of the *Authorised Version*, not familiar with 'firkins', will be surprised to learn that the action would have produced a massive 180 gallons of wine – more than enough, surely, for the largest wedding celebration! This detail alone should tell us that we have left the everyday world. There is too an odd inconsistency in Jesus' behaviour. When Mary calls

53

his attention to the catering crisis, he first expresses unconcern and declares that his hour has not yet come. Then, minutes later, he obligingly comes to the rescue. Above all, would Jesus have called upon the extraordinary powers available to him merely to save a friend from social embarrassment? This is hard to believe. Referring to Mark 2.22 (the warning not to put new wine into old skins) we can see that the intent of the tale is to contrast the stinting inadequacy of the Old Covenant with the abundant generosity of the New.

On a first reading, the case of the cripple (5.1-15) seems full of authentic and corroborative detail. Remains of the five colonnades have been found by excavators – they were destroyed when Titus captured and sacked Jerusalem in 70 A.D.; and Bethzatha (a more correct reading than Bethesda) does indeed lie to the north of the city near the Sheep Gate. But the Virgin's Spring, Gihon ('the Gusher'), is to its east near the Vale of Kidron. Its healing waters were supposed to bubble up periodically thanks to the action of an angel; but only the first comer could benefit. So, despite the early date of its first draft (the five colonnades are described as still existing), the account as it stands cannot be accepted as a plain story of fact. Once more the tale is symbolic. The thirty-eight years that the man had been crippled are also the period of Israel's wandering in the wilderness. The man is the Jewish people, whom Jesus is to rescue from their paralysis.

The healing of the nobleman's son (5.46-53) seems to be drawn from the same oral tradition as that of the centurion's servant (Matt. 8.5ff); and in fact 'royal officer' (in the service of Herod Antipas) would be a better translation of the original Greek than 'nobleman'. But several details have been changed or added. The venue is Cana, not Capernaum (some twenty miles away); the boy is now unambiguously the man's son (*huios* not *pais*); and John gives the precise time ('the seventh hour') when the fever abated. However, the main points – the healing power of faith and Jesus' welcome of the Gentiles – are the same.

John's story of the gift of sight to a man born blind (9.1-41) is reminiscent of a similar case in Mark (8.22ff). The assumption that the man's handicap was the result of sin, either his own or that of his parents, is characteristic of Jewish thought of the time. Prof. Vermes quotes a fragment from the Qumran caves relating to the cure of Nebuchadnezzar, almost certainly by Daniel: 'I was afflicted with an evil ulcer for seven years ... and a *gazer* pardoned my sins. He was a Jew.'[13] Christian theology quickly recognized what is now a platitude, that human sin is not the only cause of sickness. The symbolic element in John is the washing in the pool of Siloam. The author strains the Hebrew to make this word mean 'sent' rather than 'sending', so that the man may be represented as being baptised into Christ (the one who was sent). He thus receives illumination when all was dark to him before; and the point is emphasised by the accusation of the Pharisees of *spiritual* blindness. The detail of Siloam seems to be John's addition.

The story of Lazarus' raising from the dead (11.1-44) obviously and explicitly proclaims Jesus as the resurrection and the life; and the details prefigure his own death and burial, soon to be narrated. Lazarus had already been buried for over three days in a garden cave and the entrance covered with a stone, just as Jesus' body was to be laid in a rocky tomb, also in a garden. And sceptics have thought the parallel not accidental. They suggest that the incident was developed by the evangelist from the parable of Dives and Lazarus (Luke 16.19-25), the latter of whom enjoys eternal life in Heaven. These critics cannot have been aware of the passage in *The Secret Gospel of Mark*[14] which tells substantially the same tale with Bethany as its site.

John adds several details to its plainer narrative. 'A certain woman whose brother had died' becomes the Mary of the Mary and Martha story of Luke 10.38-42: and she in turn is identified with the woman of Luke 7.36-38 who anointed Jesus' head with myrrh and bathed his feet with her tears. 'Myrrh his sepulchre foreshows' states the Epiphany hymn. The scene of this anointing is laid by Mark (14.3-9), as well as by John, in Bethany, but in the house of Simon the leper (a leper whom Jesus had healed?), the same, no doubt, as Luke's Pharisee of that name. Mark goes straight on to tell of Judas' betrayal of his master. John's order of events at this point is thus much the same as Mark's. But he has Martha characteristically performing domestic duties, which she would hardly have done in the house of a wealthy Pharisee!

Authentic or no, these concrete details add colour and vividness to the narrative. So too does the practical Martha's suggestion that the corpse will stink, and the way Jesus 'sighs heavily and is deeply moved.' John would have made a powerful novelist. But after appreciating the drama and its spiritual overtones, we cannot evade the question, 'Has the tale a basis in actual fact?' On a practical, everyday level the answer must surely be No; for, as every First Aider knows, resuscitation must be effected immediately if a non-breathing patient is not to suffer irreparable brain damage. Resuscitated after four days, Lazarus could only have lived on as a human vegetable.

Might then the tale be regarded as a ritual myth, like that of Demeter and Persephone or the myth of Tammuz/Adonis and Aphrodite/Astarte? The latter told how the mortal youth Adonis was so handsome that the goddess Aphrodite herself fell in love with him. Unfortunately he was killed by a boar while hunting. Aphrodite (popularly called Venus) was grief-stricken; and all Nature mourned, trees shedding their leaves and flowers their blossoms. Unconsolable, the goddess even went down to the Underworld to reclaim him and bring him back to life. But the queen of that region had also taken a fancy to the youth. So at last a bargain was struck, whereby Adonis should return to Earth, but only for the spring and summer months.

Like many another, the story is a vegetation myth, dealing

with the annual withering and rebirth of crops, plants and bushes; and side by side with it went fertility rites. Women wailed for Tammuz,

> whose annual wound in Lebanon allured
> the Syrian damsels to lament his fate
> in amorous ditties all a summer's day ... (Milton. P.L. I. 447 ff)

This was a piece of sympathetic magic, their tears symbolising the hoped-for fertilising rain that would restore growth; and another was the cultivation of Adonis gardens in pot-plant containers. The plants in them were species of rapid growth, which were parched swiftly by the sun's heat.

It would not be surprising to find Christians practising mimic deaths and rebirths in initiation rituals – deaths unto sin and rebirths unto righteousness. This language is constantly on Paul's lips. We might even imagine Jesus himself employing such pageantry when admitting a newcomer into the confined inner circle of his disciples. Then we might go on to guess that gradually, in the narration of his career, these rituals became transformed into an account of an actual event whereby a particular young man, Lazarus, was resurrected from the dead.

The difficulty is that ritual myths do not develop so quickly. The lapse of centuries, even millenia, is required. Time is needed for men's memories to grow dim and for imagination to work. The New Testament period is too short. Clement of Alexandria (c.150-c.215) tells us that 'when Peter died as a martyr, Mark came over to Alexandria, bringing his own notes and those of Peter, from which he transferred to his former book the things suitable to whatever makes for progress towards knowledge (*gnosis*).'[15] This puts the insertion of this new incident into Mark's first draft not much later than 65 A.D., or roughly only 40 years after Jesus' crucifixion. The true record of events could not have become distorted so soon. Deliberate colouring of the Gospel by Gnostics did indeed occur; but Clement was well aware of this practice and vouches for the authenticity of the account in *The Secret Gospel*. It fits in naturally – or at least plausibly – after Mark 10.34.

Looking at its words again, we notice that it makes no mention of Lazarus' having been already four days in the tomb. Nor does it say specifically that the youth was dead. On the contrary it states that, as Jesus approached, a great cry was heard from the tomb. The young man was no more dead than was Jairus' daughter (Mark 5.41). His death was only an inference, although a natural one. It remained for John to add the detail of the four days to complete his symbolisation, and we have the last of the pre-resurrection 'signs' recorded in the Fourth Gospel. We should by now realise that John habitually adds corroborative detail 'to lend colour to an otherwise bald and unconvincing narrative'. The Lazarus story is not a ritual myth but the result of a deliberate remoulding of a narrative for doctrinal purposes.

Rather strangely, there is no record of Jesus' practising baptism. But it is quite possible that some kind of initiation ceremony was performed on an inner ring of 'those who were being perfected', to use Clement's phrase; and this might be what underlies the passage. Alternatively the Fourth Gospel's Lazarus story might have been developed from the account of an actual event. *The Secret Gospel's* report that Jesus displayed anger at the disciples' attempt to put the woman off is the kind of authentic detail that suggests this. It is an open question.

Early Christian missionaries recounted tales of Jesus' miracles as a proof of his divinity; and before the age of rationalism these served their purpose well. Now we live in a more sceptical time; and they have become rather a barrier to belief. The duty of the historian is, therefore, to subject them to a critical re-examination, separating the dross from the gold. Both may be found.

To us in the twentieth century only the true facts are gold, and anything else mere jetsam. John's view was different. He no more intended to write a bald chronicle of incident than did Dante in his *Divina Commedia*. In that epic poem the inhabitants of Hell are not only thirteenth century historical figures, but also and simultaneously allegorical images of certain human sins and failings. And that is their more important aspect. The same applies to John's Gospel. He saw the miraculous feats recorded of Jesus, not merely as displays of supernatural power, but as 'signs' of his nature and quality, as illustrating various facets of his person. His accounts of them are a supplement to the doctrinal discourses in the Gospel couched in narrative form.

If Jesus had performed miracles of healing on this massive scale, it is hard to understand why the Temple authorities in Jerusalem persisted in hostility towards him. It cannot be that news of the events did not travel. It would have been natural for them to recognise the feats as signs of Messianic status, and the fact that they did not argues either an incredibly open-eyed perversity on their part, or else that the Gospel accounts of the miracles are ill-founded.

But the decisive consideration is Jesus' own strategy for his mission. A series of miraculous cures would have done no more than remind the Jews of the power of God, in which they already believed. The more important task was to call people to repentance and to a new and more enlightened code of conduct. It was to this that he gave chief emphasis. And so should we.

JESUS' TEACHING

Many churchgoers will imagine that they can obtain a true enough account of Jesus' teaching from the old *Authorised Version. Sancta simplicitas!* With all its fine literary quality, that translation is at times inaccurate and based upon inferior manuscript readings. And there is a further, more subtle difficulty. Scholars believe that the message has been altered in transmission, that we have only the teaching as mediated by the early Church and used for its own instructional purposes. There was no deliberate deceit. For early Christians would have made no distinction between the words of the historical Jesus and those of the risen Christ as uttered later through inspired prophets and missionaries. The developments would have been in line with Jesus' thought, but still an embellishment on the original.

The account of Jesus' charge to the twelve apostles before sending them out on a preaching mission is a clear example (Matt. 10.17-23).[1] They are warned that they may be arrested and brought before kings and governors to testify before them and to the heathen, and that Jesus' followers must face hostility and even betrayal by their own relatives. This is looking forward to the situation under the Neronian persecution, when the Romans regarded membership of the sect as an offence in itself: the words do not apply to the situation of the first disciples in Jesus' own lifetime. Encouragement to prove steadfast in the face of hostility from government and society has been given extra authority by attribution to the Lord and Master.

A post-Crucifixion situation is also implied in the advice on how to treat a wayward brother (Matt.18.15-17). Initially an attempt must be made to settle the matter privately; but, if this fails, he is to be brought before the *congregation* (*ecclesia* – a word that can also mean 'church'.) This is an obvious anachronism. In Jesus' own day there *were* no regular congregations or churches. A few lines further on Peter is reported as having asked how often he is to forgive his brother. Why 'brother' and not 'anyone'? Perhaps Quakers' use of the words 'brethren' and 'sisters' goes back to the days of the early Church, and these verses are part of its code of conduct for its members.

Enoch Powell goes further and regards all references to children as coded language for Gentile converts.[2] The warning never to despise one of these little ones (Matt. 18.10) would then refer to the patronising attitude of the judaising faction of which we hear so much in Paul's letters. The passages make good sense if taken so. But they need not be taken so; and, since they make perfectly good sense taken literally, as they stand, this reinterpretation seems an excess of ingenuity.

The change to a later audience seems to have led to adaptation of the details of some of Jesus' parables. A good example is that of the doorkeeper (Mark 13.33-37, Luke 12.33-35, cf Matt. 24.42). The German scholar Jeremias[3] argues that this was originally told only of a single servant instructed to keep watch while his master was away at a banquet. In Luke we find that the command has been given to *all* the servants, and in Mark 13.34 these are entrusted with authority to manage affairs, as if the master were going away on a long journey. So the *hour* of the master's return is altered to its *day*; and finally we have the prospect of the faithful servants rewarded with an invitation to sit down to a meal served by the master himself – a very democratic procedure for those times! The suspicion arises that alterations and additions have been made to suit the situation of the primitive Church, when Christ's second coming was unexpectedly delayed and the faithful were urged to remain alert and watchful, assured that their fidelity would reap its due reward. Jesus' original point was simply the need for readiness against the day of judgment.

The needs of preaching to the converted might also lead to the conversion of parables into allegories. Typically a parable is designed to inculcate a single truth or moral. In an allegory each detail of the tale has its own meaning and significance. One knows how preachers today strive to extract and point to every possible meaning that a Gospel reading may hold. Their first century predecessors seem to have been no different; and how parable could become allegory is well illustrated by the one of the Great Supper. *The Gospel of Thomas* No. 64 gives what is probably the earliest version:

> A man had received visitors. And when he had prepared the dinner, he sent his servants to invite the guests. He went to the first one and said to him, 'My master invites you'. He said, 'I have claims against some merchants. They are coming to me this evening. I must go and give them my orders. I ask to be excused from the dinner.' He went to another and said to him, 'My master has invited you.' He said to him, 'I have just bought a house and am required for the day. I shall not have any spare time.' He went to another and said to him, 'My master invites you.' He said to him, 'My friend is going to get married, and I am to prepare the banquet. I shall not be able to come. I ask to be excused from the dinner.' He went to another and said to him, 'My master invites you.' He said to him, 'I have just bought a farm, and I am on my way to collect the rent, I shall not be able to come. I ask to be excused.' The servant returned and said to his master, 'Those whom you invited to the dinner have asked to be excused.' The master said to his servant, 'Go outside to the streets, and bring back these you happen to meet, so that they may dine. Business men and merchants will not enter the places of my Father.'

In Matthew (22.1-14) the man has become a king (i.e. God), the dinner a marriage feast for the king's son (Christ), and the single servant a number of servants (the prophets). These are not merely spurned, but attacked and killed. So the king sends troops to kill the murderers and set their town on fire (Hell?). We have come far from the original plan of a social gathering. Still keeping this original context, Luke (14.16-4) divides the late invitees into two classes: (a) the dropouts in the streets (the publicans and sinners) and (b) those along the hedgerows and highways (the Gentiles). Matthew at least thus transforms the original parable into an allegory of the plan of salvation. When first told it had only two main points: to warn Jesus' opponents not to reject his mission and to vindicate his consorting with tax-gatherers and sinners.

Matthew's footnote to this parable, where one guest is reproved for his lack of a wedding garment, has puzzled readers. How could such an expectation reasonably be entertained of a tramp or vagrant? N. Perrin explains that it was the Jewish custom to issue two invitations, one an advance warning and another a reminder more nearly specifying the time, so that wise guests would be ready and waiting. The moral, in the words of a familiar hymn, would then be 'For the great day thyself prepare.' It is really a separate parable, tacked on to the other because of its wedding context.

Jeremias also rejects as inauthentic the allegorical explanations of the parable of the sower (Mark 4.1-20). Asked for its meaning, Jesus says that people vary in their receptivity to the Gospel as do soils to seed. Jeremias regards the passage as a later addition, though with reluctance, on grounds of style. But to apply this test of authorship to so short a passage is hazardous, especially when the interpretation fits the narrative like a glove. It helps to appreciate the parable to know that in Jesus' day sowing would precede ploughing. This was done with a primitive instrument that did not dig deep, so that there was every chance for some seeds to fall on stony ground, and some where there was no depth of earth. To that extent the details reflect the contemporary scene. But there is no seed at all which bears a hundredfold! That detail is given to indicate the glorious future that awaited Jesus' ministry despite its small beginnings.

Besides being wary of the early Christians' penchant for converting parables into allegories, we have to take care not to do the same ourselves – in the tale of Dives and Lazarus (Luke 16.19-31), for instance. We are not to suppose that Dives was consigned to Hell and torment merely because of his wealth and affluence, nor (despite the saying that the poor would inherit the earth) that the beggar Lazarus was sent to Abraham's bosom merely because of his destitution. Jesus was making use of an Egyptian folk tale with a significant addition of his own. In this Dives is made to plead that Lazarus may be sent to warn his five brothers before they share his fate. The stern answer is that those who ignored Moses and the prophets would not be impressed even if someone returned from the dead. This is the sole lesson of the tale. It is a nice question whether Jesus was referring to his own future resurrection or speaking more generally of miracles in vivid form.

There is no such ambiguity in the parable of the sheep and the goats (Matt. 25.31-46). There the prospect of the Son of Man coming in his glory can only refer to Jesus' own resurrection and second coming (referred to fashionably by scholars as the Parousia). The language is explicit: 'When *I* was hungry, you gave *me* food . . . (and) anything you did for my brothers here you did for *me*.' Visitors to Greece and the Near East will understand that sheep and goats more nearly resemble each other there than in the British Isles. There is a similar initial likeness between wheat and tares (Matt. 13.24-30). The latter (*lolium temulentum*) is at first indistinguishable from wheat, yet highly poisonous. In both of these parables the Judge will decide on the basis of behaviour and its effects; and, whether Jesus believed in a Hell or not, he is certainly represented as believing in a judgment.

The word 'brothers' in the first of these parables might support

Enoch Powell in his belief that it is a composition of the early Church. Yet it is difficult to suggest a better alternative term.

In the parable of the foolish virgins (Matt. 25.1-12), charged to escort the bridegroom, the reference to the Parousia is not so certain. The Messiah was not habitually referred to as the bridegroom in Jewish prophecy, although Jesus did use this metaphor of himself (Mark 2.19). A nocturnal wedding ceremony is a surprise to modern readers; but it would not be strange in Palestine, where even today the appearance of the groom at the bride's father's home is the climax of the celebrations and comes well into evening. This explains the injunction 'to keep the lamps all bright and trim the golden flame'. Non-Christian scholars believe that Jesus was merely warning of the need for readiness at the time of judgment, and not necessarily forecasting his own second coming. There is a similar doubt with regard to most of the Judgment parables.

Once more Enoch Powell assigns the passage to a post-Crucifixion context. 'The oil is the supply of converts to keep the churches shining in the world; and the moral is: no converts, no entry into the kingdom (of heaven).'[4] This is a clear enhancement; and the point is certainly one which might have occurred to a first century missionary. Yet this does not exclude the possibility that the parable was first told by Jesus himself.

Knowledge of ancient customs also aids understanding of the parable of the unjust steward (Luke 16.1-8). Called upon to present his accounts, the man practises a deceit which seems today too transparent for belief, simply bidding the various debtors re-write their bonds. We have to realise that the original IOUs would have been made out in their own handwriting by way of proof of the amounts involved. An allegorical interpretation of the tale would be particularly disastrous in this instance, since 'the lord' who commended the dishonest steward is probably Jesus in person. The moral is only the need to take action against the day of reckoning. The means is a separate matter.

This theme also plays a part in the parable of the talents (Matt. 25.14-30 and Luke 19.12-27). Misinterpretation is traditional, so that 'talent' today means only 'inherited expertise or aptitude'. In the ancient world a talent was a sum of money, with the same emotional impact as £1 million in the 1930s or even £1 billion today. Luke more modestly writes of *mnae*, or 1/60th of that sum; and he has also conflated the original parable in Matthew with another. Matthew tells of 'a man' going abroad and entrusting his servants with various sums to manage during his absence, and rewarding them or punishing them on his return according to their performance. Luke alters 'the man' to a nobleman going off to claim a kingdom, as in fact Archelaus did on the death of Herod the Great; and again, as in history, some of his people send a delegation of protest. For this disloyalty they pay with their lives. It looks as if the primitive Church grafted on to Jesus' parable one of its own composition holding out the prospect of the punishment of its enemies at Jesus' second coming.

The obvious moral in Matthew is that we should not be idle or unprofitable servants. But idle or unprofitable in what way? Enoch Powell is almost certainly right to answer 'in bringing in new converts into the Faith.'[5] Without this interpretation it is hard to find a Christian message in what, on the face of it, seems a commendation of profiteering; and this would also explain why this parable is placed next to the one about the foolish virgins in Matthew's text. We should remember that in the early days of the Church it used to be made clear to new adherents that they were expected to bring others into the fold.

Jeremias believes that the parable refers to Jesus' own times and takes it as a warning to the Pharisees and others of the religious establishment, who had been entrusted with the Law and the prophets and had failed to make proper use of that trust.

It was to such opponents of Jesus, he thinks, that his parables were mainly addressed, and that a recollection that they were among the original audience will often reveal additional meanings. An example is that of the labourers in the vineyard (Matt. 20.1-16). The primary moral is that is possible for latecomers to gain full salvation even at the eleventh hour; but the claim of those who had borne the labour and heat of the day that they should receive a proportionately greater reward seems reasonable and demands an answer. Their complaint reflects the tendency of the Pharisees to view the Old Covenant in a contractual light, whereby Yahweh's blessing on his people depended on their first fulfilling the demands of the Torah or Law. Jesus was insisting that the rewards of Heaven could come through God's grace, freely given. The parable anticipates Paul's discussion of the relative merits of faith and works in his letter to the Romans.

There is a similar dual import in the parable of the prodigal son (Luke 15.11-32). It was common for younger sons to go abroad to seek their fortunes in Jesus' day, just as British younger sons often tried their luck in the colonies in Victorian times; and not all struck gold. But this was a particularly bad case. Not only had the young man spent his substance on riotous living, but by becoming a swineherd he had broken Jewish taboos. He thus rendered himself a Gentile and a non-person. To the average Jewish father he was effectively dead. Yet on his return home he is more than forgiven: his welcome is lavish, recalling Pharaoh's treatment of Joseph when appointing him his grand vizier. He has bestowed on him a ring, a special robe and a golden chain; and he is given meat (the fatted calf) to eat – a food reserved for special occasions. Like the first group of labourers, the elder brother voices the claims of previous service – and none too politely. He is told in effect that there is more joy in Heaven over one repentant sinner than over ninety-nine just persons, and that God would freely forgive.

This was a new thought for the Jews. Sin and debt were the same word in Aramaic (as we can see in the alternative versions of the Lord's prayer); and any transgression involved a debt to God, payable normally by sacrifice or by almsgiving. The idea of God's free forgiveness was a new conception.

The parable also illustrates an important additional feature of Jesus' ministry: his welcome to tax-gatherers and sinners. Jeremias and Perrin both think that this was symbolised by a table-fellowship of common meals, and that it was these that led to the charge that he was a wine-bibber (Matt. 11.19). These love-feasts seem to have been a part of the early Christian life, and must be what Paul is referring to in 1 Corinthians 11.17 ff. They were apparently 'bring and share' occasions; for Paul speaks of each of the Corinthians being in a hurry to eat his own, and of one person going empty while another has too much to drink. The custom is also mentioned by the younger Pliny in a letter to the Emperor Trajan.[6] The communal repast he describes took place after and separately from the church service, and was, he implies, unmarred by cannibalism! (Distorted accounts of the communion service and of the doctrine of hell-fire had caused Christians to be thought guilty of this and of incendiarism.) As agents of the occupying power, tax-collectors were regarded by Jews as traitors and quislings, whose own actions had made them Gentiles (Matt. 18.17); and Jesus also would have become a Gentile in the eyes of many strict Jews through his association with them. Otherwise, Perrin[7] believes, the high priests and Sanhedrin would never have handed him over, a fellow Jew, to the foreign governor.

In view of this it is a surprise that so great a scholar as Prof. Vermes claims that Jesus never envisaged a systematic mission to the Gentiles. If this were so, he would have been breaking with the developing thought of Judaism. As early as the seventh century B.C. the author of Genesis has God promise to Abraham: 'In thee shall all the nations of the earth be blessed'

(Gen. 22.18). Then in the next century Deutero-Isaiah predicts that God's servant will bring forth judgment to the Gentiles (42.1), and imagines him speaking to his servant and saying: 'It is too light a task for you to restore the tribes of Jacob ... I will make you a light to the nations, to be my salvation to earth's farthest bounds.' In the late sixth century the prophet Zechariah pictures a Jew bringing in ten spiritual captives, who plead for admission to Judaism (8.23); and these proselytes are envisaged as keeping the Law punctiliously, so that 'mine house shall be called a house of prayer for all peoples' (Isaiah 56.7). Finally we have the testimony of the 'Testament of the Twelve Patriarchs', written by a Pharisee between 109 and 107 B.C., whose author holds that not only Jews, but all the Gentiles, will be saved.

It would be strange for Jesus to have gone back on this tradition; and the accounts of his healing the centurion's servant and the daughter of the Syro-phoenician woman suggest quite the contrary. The parable of the wicked tenants (Matt. 21.33-46, Mark 12.1-11, Luke 20.29-31) suggests the same conclusion. An absentee landlord (i.e. God) leaves the tenants in charge of his estate; but when he sends servants (the prophets) to collect the rent, they are beaten or killed; and finally, when he sends his son (Jesus) in the hope that he will command more respect, the tenants decide to kill him in the belief that the estate will then be theirs. Jesus declares that the landlord will bring the wicked tenants to a bad end and hand over the estate to other tenants. To the dropouts of Israel or to the Gentiles? The Jews' exclamation, 'God forbid', suggests the latter; and this identification finds support in Matt. 8.11, where we are told that many will come from east and west to feast with Abraham, Isaac and Jacob in the Kingdom of Heaven, while those who were born to the Kingdom will be driven out into the dark.[8]

We wonder how the tenants could be so naive as to imagine that murder could leave them in possession of the lands. But the parable is true to the social and economic situation of the time.

The whole of the upper Jordan valley and a large part of the Galilean uplands were owned by foreign and absentee landlords, naturally unpopular with the native peasants; and retribution for violent seizure would have been slow to come. The fact of this background to the tale confirms that this parable is one of Jesus' own, and not a composition of the primitive church. The churches established by Paul lay in Greece and Asia Minor (the modern Turkey), where the circumstances would have been different.

How faithfully the Gospels reflect the life of the times may also be seen in the prayers of the Pharisee and the tax-gatherer (Luke 18.9-14). The Pharisee's self-righteous complacency is paralleled in a first century A.D. prayer in the Jewish Talmud:

> I thank thee, O Lord, my God, that thou hast given me my lot with those who sit in the seat of learning, and not with those who sit at the street corners . . . I am early to work on the words of the Torah, and they are early to work on things of no moment . . . I weary myself and profit thereby, while they weary themselves to no profit . . . I run towards the life of the Age to Come, while they run towards the pit of destruction.

So Jesus was not exaggerating. He was more than fair, making his Pharisee fast twice, not merely once, in the week and paying tithes on *all* his possessions – including farm produce that should have been taxed already. There is the same point as in the parable of the prodigal son, that no man is good enough to *earn* salvation. This comes to all through grace. Jesus' objection to the Pharisees was not only one of moral attitude but theological.

Deeper issues are also involved in Jesus' disputes with some extreme Pharisees over Sabbath observance and ritual purity (Mark 2.1-3.6). In the first, that of the man with the withered arm, Jesus was in line with mainstream Jewish thought, which recognised that the question of healing on the Sabbath was a matter of common sense priorities.[9] Perhaps also ordinary Jews would have washed their hands before meals only when hygienically necessary, and the objectors were nitpicking. When we come to the third instance, when the disciples were criticised for hand-winnowing ears of corn as they walked through the fields, we wonder what such exalted personages as the Pharisees were doing deep in the countryside. Prof. Vermes regards the tale as 'didactic rather than historical',[10] and designed to make the point that saving life from starvation overrode the claims of formal religious observance. If so, the Gospel-writers could surely have devised a tale with more verisimilitude. A more likely explanation is that the Pharisees had been charged to keep Jesus under observation, as they had previously done John the Baptist (Matt. 3.7). This would be very probable if Jesus had made an attack on the Temple money-changers early in his career, as John records (2.12-17).

All these cases involved a basic question of principle – whether morality consisted merely in observance of a miscellaneous collection of 'Do's' and 'Don'ts', based wholly on tradition, or whether all these dictates were based upon a central principle. The same question arises when modern politicians claim that their private behaviour is their own affair so long as they perform their public duties with efficiency. Implicitly Jesus denied that ethical conduct could be split up into compartments in this way. He claimed that what was crucial was a person's general moral stance. If that were sound, detailed rules of conduct were unnecessary; for a right spirit within a man would direct the whole of his life.

This regard for the spirit rather than for the letter of the law is both more lenient and more exacting. There is no real contradiction between the two. And this thought helps to explain some words in the Sermon on the Mount which superficially seem at variance with Jesus' general stance: 'Think not that I am come to destroy the Law: I am not come to destroy, but to fulfil' (Matt. 5.17). With this introduction Jesus proceeds to take one after another of the Ten Commandments and demand a higher standard, insisting that a person's moral state does not depend solely on negative abstention from lawbreaking. Even our thoughts have to be kept under control. Perverted imaginings corrupt no less than actual misdeeds, and will come to a reckoning in God's judgment, which Jesus more than once predicted. In similar vein the Psalmist (51.6) wrote 'Thou desirest truth in the inward parts'. Linked up with this is the advice to do good by stealth (Matt. 6.2) and not to make a parade of virtue. Charitable giving must not be trumpeted, nor fasting signalled by sackcloth and ashes; and prayers are best made alone in a private room.

Two injunctions from this section, to turn the other cheek and to love our enemies, require some commentary. Striking a person on the right cheek could only be done with a back-handed slap, and was a formal insult, like throwing down the gauntlet – not a spontaneous act of violence and battery; and the advice to turn the other cheek was a plea not to stand rigidly upon one's dignity and adopt a legalistic attitude. It is not necessarily a text to support a political policy of passive resistance.

The same applies to the oft quoted 'Love your enemies' (Matt. 5.44). The Greek word *echthroi* here is used always of personal enemies, individuals who inspire dislike, either by their appearance or behaviour. National foes are *polemioi* (whence 'polemical'). And the love Jesus is speaking of is *agape*, not *eros* (sexual desire) or *philia* (friendly feeling). *Agape* describes, not an emotion, but a deliberate disposition of the will. It can refer to acts of good will done almost against the inclination – to giving first aid, for instance, to a wounded and grounded enemy airman who has just bombed your town. This kind of love involves works of supererogation.

An example of this is the injunction to go the extra mile (Matt. 5.39-41). The reference is to the Roman practice of requisitioning not merely goods, but services and labour, and here to the order to carry a soldier's pack a statutory mile. A Christian will do more than his legal obligation. Advice not to stand upon the letter of the law is also the advice being given in 'If a man sues you for your tunic, let him have your cloak as well.' We need to understand that in ancient Palestine ordinary wear consisted of two garments: cloak and under-tunic, and that the law (Deut. 24.12f) forbade the stripping down of any debtor to more than his cloak. Again Jesus is urging people not to 'throw the rule book' but to deal in an amicable way. He is not advocating nudism!

The Sermon on the Mount reads like a connected discourse. But this structure is more probably the work of Matthew than of Jesus himself. Its eminent quotability indicates that it is composed of a number of disconnected sayings uttered on different occasions. Unlike the parables these would not be susceptible of alteration, and we can be confident that they are authentic. In so far as they echo the parables, they confirm that the latter convey the original message. By and large the teaching is the same.

This is certainly so with regard to the 'hard sayings', which seem almost a barrier to faith. Bidden to sell all that he had, give to the poor, and then follow Jesus, who had nowhere to lay his head, the rich young ruler not unnaturally jibbed (Matt. 19.16-19). And Jesus seems harsh and uncompromising towards the would-be disciple who asked for leave first to bury his father before joining Jesus' following (Matt. 8.21 f). 'Let the dead bury the dead' replied Jesus. Some have argued that the man's father was still alive and well, and the plea merely an excuse for procrastination; but we are not told so. Hardest of all are the words of Matt. 10.32-39: 'I have come to set a man against his father, a daughter against her mother ... No man is worthy of me who cares for father or mother more than for me.' It is true that it is often morally more difficult to take a theological stand against a near relative than against an outsider; but the language seems abrupt and heartless, and the preaching of the Gospel would be easier in its absence. That these sayings have been preserved is an indication of the essential honesty of the Gospel-writers.

Clearly, if Christianity were to involve the whole population becoming wandering nomads, the life of the world could not be carried on. No more could it be if all made themselves eunuchs, i.e. remained celibate. The explanation must be that for the inner ring of his disciples Jesus prescribed a specially strict regime like that of the later monkish orders. They were an élite, and were given extra theological training and instruction, whereas the mass of the people were given teaching only in the popular form of parables (Mar 4.11). We might know more of this if *The Secret Gospel of Mark* had survived in full. A parallel may be found in the teaching of the Greek philosopher Plato, who wrote his dialogues only for popular consumption and contended that his profoundest doctrines could not be imparted by those means.

But, while requiring a vow of poverty only from the inner group of his disciples, Jesus repeatedly insisted on the perils of the acquisitive pursuit of wealth for mankind in general. It is the poor who are blessed (Luke 6.21), and it is as hard for a rich man to enter the Kingdom of Heaven as for a camel to pass through a needle's eye (Matt. 19.24). 'Lay not up for yourselves treasures upon earth . . . but lay up for yourselves treasures in Heaven (Matt. 6.19). 'Ye cannot serve God and Mammon' (Matt. 6.24). Money-making must not become a priority, and all else must take second place to the salvation of the soul; for this is the pearl of great price (Matt. 13.45-46), which a wise merchant will part with all his other goods to gain.

Jesus pursues the theme with stern vehemence. 'If your hand is your undoing, cut it off;[11] it is better for you to enter into life maimed than to keep both hands and go to hell . . . And if it is your eye that causes you to sin, tear it out; it is better to enter into the Kingdom of God with one eye than to keep both eyes and be thrown into hell.'

We come here upon an aspect of Jesus' teaching which led to the Gnostic heresy and to the extreme asceticism of monks, who cut themselves off from the wicked world to live alone in the desert – 'fugitive and cloistered virtue, afraid of its own enemy'. It cannot have been Jesus' intention to recommend the hermitage as a means to salvation of the soul, or to portray the material world as wholly and incurably evil. That (Gnostic) view was contrary both to Christian and Jewish thought. God had created the world of sense along with the world of spirit, and it must therefore be good.

But Jesus was given to vivid and rhetorical exaggeration so as to drive his message home. The example of the camel and the needle's eye has already been quoted, and his assertion that faith can move mountains is familiar. We shall soon come to other instances. There was a danger here of misinterpretation – indeed more than a danger. Reading that some had made themselves eunuchs for the sake of the Kingdom, the scholar Origen took the words literally as a prescription for discipleship and had himself castrated! It is even possible that Jesus' words at the Last Supper ('This is my body') were merely metaphorical, and that the doctrine of transsubstantiation is an embellishment by Paul. (This, of course, is not to say that the bread and wine at the Eucharist may not be *effectively* Christ's body and blood.)

In the *Authorised Version* of Mat. 6.25 ff ('Take no thought for your life, what ye shall eat or what ye shall drink.') we have rhetorical exaggeration compounded with mistranslation. The Greek words *me merimnate* mean only 'Do not be anxious . . .' But then, so as to make his point colourfully, Jesus goes on with 'Behold the fowls of the air; for they sow not, neither do they reap, nor gather into barns; yet your heavenly father feedeth them.' This is to depart from strict accuracy. In fact birds do spend a large part of the day in search of nourishment, and herbivores most of the day in grazing or masticating. It cannot have been Jesus' intent that men should merely wait for food to drop into their hands; but his words could easily discourage a proper prudence.

There is also less substance than poetry in the succeeding verses: 'And why take ye thought for raiment? Consider the lilies of the field, how they grow; they toil not, neither do they spin. And yet I say unto you that even Solomon in all his glory was not arrayed like one of these.' Unlike men, plants[12] have no need of clothing. Merely to have told his audience that material satisfactions should take second place to spiritual needs would not have had the same impact; but prosaic truth has been sacrificed for dramatic effect.

Jesus instances God's care for the birds again in Matt 10.29ff: 'Are not two sparrows sold for a farthing? And one of them shall not fall to the ground without your Father ... Fear not therefore; ye are of more value than many sparrows.' This idea of the fatherhood of God was a new concept. In the Old Testament God is indeed portrayed as the creator and begetter of the Jewish people, but he is still a somewhat distant and regal figure. To Jesus his fatherhood is personal and individual. God is both caring and forgiving, and it is in virtue of his close relationship with mankind that he knows the secrets of human hearts. In line with this perception Jesus regularly addresses God with the colloquial word 'Abba'; but this is still not so familiar as our word 'Daddy', as some writers and preachers have imagined.[13] A better comparison would be with the Victorian 'Papa' – affectionate, but also respectful.

Mutual affection inspires trust; and this is the point in Mark 10.14f: 'Suffer the little children to come unto me, and forbid them not: for of such is the Kingdom of God ... Whosoever shall not receive the Kingdom of God as a little child, he shall not enter therein.' The quality in children that Jesus is recommending is their trustfulness and reliance upon their parents. Adults in turn should show the same faith in God (Matt. 7.11).

The point about children in Matt. 11.25-27 is a different one. 'I thank thee, Father, because thou hast hid these things from the wise and prudent, and hast revealed them unto babes.' The knowledge in question is the knowledge of the Gnostics – not that of scholastic learning or deep erudition, but that of direct insight; and the suggestion is that this is not confined to the intellectually gifted but is available to all. So children can have as direct an awareness of God as have adults. There is an echo of this thought in *The Gospel of Thomas* No. 4: 'The man old in days will not hesitate to ask a small child seven days old about the place of life, and he will live. For many who are first will become last.' There is another echo in *Thomas* No. 46: 'Among those born of women there is no one superior to John the Baptist ... Yet I have said, whichever of you comes to be a child will be acquainted with his (God's) Kingdom and will become superior to John.' This helps us to interpret Matt.11. 11: 'Never has there appeared on earth a mother's son greater than John the Baptist, and yet the least in the Kingdom of Heaven is greater than he.' If all these sayings attributed to Jesus are authentic, we have a strand in his teaching which is only poorly represented in the canonical Gospels, and which may have later encouraged Gnosticism.

For this reason it is worthwhile to have another look at Mcgregor Ross' interpretation of *The Gospel of Thomas*. As already remarked, it is impossible that Jesus should have used such a Freudian term as 'the Ego'. But it is very possible that he should have had a similar conception, and that he should, like Plato with his theory of the tripartite soul, have insisted that its various elements should run in harness as a team. Plato had need of great ingenuity to expound his philosophy in the Greek language; and Hebrew and Aramaic were even less adapted for the expression of philosophic and theological thought. It is, therefore, credible enough that Jesus should have had to proceed by way of hints and examples, using 'the male' for 'the masculine principle or tendency'. And here we should note that it is men, and not women, who have been responsible for most of the violence in the world. There are few female soccer hooligans.

This masculine principle is restless and unconservative, and without it we should have fewer fruitful initiatives in the world. 'Divine discontent' is needed for progress. But it needs to be directed and controlled, and not allowed to play too large a part. Otherwise it will obscure our spiritual vision, and we shall lose touch with the divine. We need to achieve what Freud called an integrated personality.

Children have the advantage, according to McGregor Ross' interpretation, of being born without this Ego. It is something which develops. 'Heaven lies about us in our infancy.' There is no such thing as Original Sin, and we have in our earliest years a more direct awareness of God. Orthodox theology takes a different view. 'In sin hath my mother conceived me', wrote the Psalmist.

Misdirected, the Ego will turn to the pursuit of wealth and riches. Not that this is the only manifestation of a misdirected Ego: but it is a very large and significant part, turning the eye of the soul away from God; and perhaps this is the point that the poet T.S. Eliot had in mind when he wrote:

> To possess what you do not possess you must go by a way of dispossession.

The condition of the beatific vision is an emptying of vain desires.

Something like this might well have played a part in Jesus' teaching. But this interpretation of *The Gospel of Thomas* is doubtfully the whole story. Such an ethic would have easily been 'understanded of the people.' It would be no secret gospel, accessible only to the elect. We need to look further; and W.T.

Stace's book, *Religion and the Modern Mind* is particularly illuminating.

He notes a significant agreement in thought and language among the mystics of all the world's religious faiths, Christian and others. 'What is common to all of (the utterances of these mystics) is the assertion that there is a kind of experience, a way of experiencing the world, in which the distinctions between one thing and another, including the distinction between the subject and the object, self and not self, are abolished, overcome, transcended, so that all the *different* things in the world become one, become identical with one another (p. 239f). In such an experience the mind has necessarily passed beyond time and space. For time and space are the very conditions of division, separation, multiplicity, contrast. (p. 241)... The vision transcends intellection and is quite ineffable – no words can describe it, 'because all words depend on distinctions between one thing and another.' (p. 40).

In the light of this, the words of *Thomas* No. 22 become more intelligible: 'When you make the two one, and when you make the inside like the outside, and the above like the below ... then you will enter the Kingdom.'

'The experience', Stace goes on (p. 48f), 'also has the character of *eternality*. For since time and space are the principles of division, and the experience is of divisionless unity, it is therefore "above time and space". Even if the ecstatic vision lasts only a moment ... yet that moment, as seen from within itself, is timeless and eternal. For this is the meaning of eternity. It does not mean unending time, but timelessness.'... 'It would seem that the true religious vision is possible only to a few extraordinary men. For the great mystic is rarer even than the great poet' (p. 55).

The situation of the ordinary man, believing in the evidence only of his intellect and in the teachings of science, is analogous to that of a person seeing a mirage in the desert. However much we assure him that there is in fact no such pool or grove of trees where he imagines he sees one, he cannot easily believe us. Similarly with regard to the saint or mystic and his beatific vision. He may assure us that all is one; but our eyes, our intellects, and even the language itself tell us differently.

Stace's chapter also sheds light on the poetry of T.S. Eliot. Eliot is not wilfully obscure, but is seeking to explain matters with the utmost clarity. The apparent riddles are almost literally true.

>   to apprehend
> the point of intersection of the timeless
> with time is an occupation for the saint ...
>
> For most of us there is only the unattended
> moment, the moment in and out of time.
> *(The Dry Salvages)*

> I can only say, *there* we have been: but I cannot say where.
> And I cannot say, how long, for that is to place it in time.
>   *(Burnt Norton)*

There is need for more research on this. But what is clear is that *The Gospel of Thomas* presents the Kingdom of God, not as a new world order, but as a spiritual state within the individual person. We get the same impression from Jesus' reply to the lawyer who agreed so heartily as to which was the greatest commandment (Mark 12.34). 'You are not far from the Kingdom of God.' *The Authorised Version* of Luke 17.21 has him speaking similarly to a Pharisee. Asked 'When will the Kingdom come?' Jesus answers, 'The Kingdom of God is within you.'

But this unfortunately is a translation from an inferior manuscript, and a more correct version is 'The Kingdom of God is among you.' In other words the Kingdom had already arrived in Jesus own activity and mission, and Matthew (12.28) reports him as claiming his successful exorcisms as proof of this. Some Pharisees had been arguing that it was through the aid of Beelzebub that he cast out devils. Jesus makes a twofold reply: that this would imply that Satan's realm was divided against itself – an obvious nonsense; and that the exorcisms indicated that a stronger power than Satan was now at work in the world. It is not quite clear whether this stronger power was Jesus himself or God working through him.

Luke (11.20) gives a fuller version: 'When a strong man fully armed is on guard over his castle his possessions are safe. But when someone stronger comes upon him and overpowers him, he carries off the arms and armour on which the man had relied and divides the plunder.' Some scholars identify Jesus with the 'someone stronger'.

The two conceptions of the Kingdom of God, as an inner and spiritual state and as a new development initiated by Jesus' teaching and ministry, are not necessarily at variance with one another or mutually exclusive. His own appearance as God's spokesman and his followers' acceptance of the message were both signs that God had once more intervened decisively in History, were twin aspects of the same cosmic event. And a greater, more splendid consummation was in prospect, to which Jesus' ministry was related as seed-time to harvest. This is the meaning most readers give to the words 'The Kingdom of God is at hand' (Mark 1.15); and they are not mistaken. And with the book of the Revelation of St John the Divine in mind they commonly imagine this as Jesus' second coming after his resurrection and ascension and as the end of the world of Time.

Yet on this last point Prof. Sanders[14] believes that the average reader is in error. 'Jesus did not expect the end of the world in the sense of destruction of the cosmos. He expected a divine, transforming miracle.' The world was not to be destroyed but redeemed. The twelve apostles were to sit on twelve thrones judging the twelve tribes of Israel – twelve once more, for the ten tribes lost in 721B.C. with the fall of Samaria would be restored. (Matt. 19.27-29). 'I make all things new' (Rev. 21.5).

Along with the Book of Revelation the general reader commonly has in mind Jesus' prophecies recorded in Mark 13 and the parallel passages in Matthew 24.1-36 and in Luke 21.5-36. These eschatological discourses (as scholars call them) have given rise to much learned discussion. Some writers adopt the view that Jesus mistakenly expected the end of the world in the near future, others that he set no limit on the coming of the End. Others again have maintained that there was no parousia (Second Coming) element in his teaching, and that much of the chapters are editorial prophecies after the event. If so, Luke at least did a poor job. 'When you see Jerusalem encircled by armies . . . those who are in the city must leave it' (Luke 21.21-22). Surely too late for such action!

Mark's passage begins with Jesus prophesying the destruction of the Temple. And this is something he may well have done. Given the temper of his people, the forecast would have demanded little perspicacity. For the same reason it would have been easy to guess that there were to be more Messianic claimants. There had already been one, Judas the Galilean, in 6 A.D., and there were to be four more before the failure of the Jewish revolt in 70 A.D. These are things which Jesus could easily have predicted; and he is recorded as having done so again just before his crucifixion, telling the women of Jerusalem to weep, not for him but for themselves and their future fate. 'If they do these things in a green tree, what shall be done in the dry?' (Luke 23.31). The accents here are not Luke's, but Jesus' own. There is almost certainly an authentic core to Mark's chapter.

But it is also probably a case of the evangelist 'remembering with advantages' and with the aid of later history. In the birth pangs of the new age, we read, 'nation will rise up against nation.' This seems a clear reference to the year 69 A.D., which saw not only civil war between rival armies but nationalist risings in

Judaea and on the Rhine. And there had been a similar rebellion in Gaul the previous year. The prophecy of earthquakes in the same verse might have been made after the event in the light of those occurring at Laodicaea in 60 A.D. and at Pompeii in 63 A.D. The description of the abomination of desolation usurping a place which is not his (v.14) is a more complicated matter. In the original draft of the Gospel the words were probably a covert description of the emperor Gaius' plan to have a colossal statue of himself set up in the Holy of Holies in 40 A.D. Such desecration roused the whole Jewish nation to resistance; and, with more understanding than his master, the governor Petronius dallied as much as he dared in the execution of the scheme. The delay irritated the emperor, and Petronius' own head was in danger. But at the last minute a crisis was averted by Gaius' assassination. In 70 A.D. the victorious Titus actually did set foot in the inner sanctum. But he, of course, was not a thing, but a man. So a slight alteration was made to the text, substituting a masculine for a neuter participle in 'standing'. It is a nice question whether the change was made by the original author or by a later well-meaning scribe.

These, however, may all be dismissed as instances of 'mere corroborative detail'. Essentially Mark is honest; and his honesty is proved by the existence of verse 31 ('the present generation will live to see it all'). The apostles did not live to see a Second Coming: the prophecy remained unrealised. And that it should have been recorded is an indication of Mark's true sincerity. The words have always been an embarrassment to the Church, and their preservation is an index of the good faith of early and later Christians.

A few lines above comes the forecast of 'the Son of Man coming in the clouds with great power and glory.' The obvious and natural interpretation is of Jesus' own return after his ascension. Those who think otherwise put their trust in the work of some pre-war German scholars. These argued that there existed in Jewish apocalyptic writings the conception of a transcendent pre-existent heavenly being, the Son of Man, whose coming to earth as judge would be a major feature of the drama of the end of Time, and that it was to this that Jesus was referring, and not to himself.

The words in question are a reminiscence of a verse in the Book of Daniel (7.13), and the surrounding passage there has inspired Christian hymnody with references to God as the Ancient of Days, 'pavilioned in splendour and girded with praise.' When written, its chapters referred to the Maccabean revolt against the Jews' then overlord, Antiochus Epiphanes, and were designed to encourage the Jewish fighters with the thought that their sufferings would eventually be rewarded. But later secondary meanings were seen, and the passage became the fountain head of a stream of apocalyptic. Examples are the pseudepigraphic writings of I Enoch and IV Ezra. (These are now available only in an out-of-print and weighty tome, but Bertrand Russell's *History of Western Philosophy* p. 337ff. gives a useful summary.) Some of them at least seem not to have been composed before the second century A.D., and are therefore not relevant to Jesus' teaching. And Norman Perrin,[15] who goes into the subject deeply, believes that there *was* no recognised figure of a Son of Man in the Jewish thought of Jesus' lifetime for him to have referred to or identified himself with.

It appears, then, that the obvious interpretation is the right one. In this eschatological chapter 'Son of Man' (*bar nasha*) is, as usually, simply code for 'I' or 'me', and the discourse by Jesus does indeed contain a prophecy of his Second Coming (a doctrine not likely to have been invented by the early Church). The echoes of Old Testament writings within it are due merely to his having employed the half-remembered imagery of remembered scriptures.

Two consequences ensue. A minor one is that some scholars should be less sceptical over references to the Second Coming in the parables. The more important is that Jesus had by his last week come to regard himself as more than an ordinary man. If he did not do so at the start of his mission, then his successful exorcisms and miracles of healing would have encouraged this belief. Pace the author of *Honest to God*,[16] he *did* make claims for himself; and there is for us no evading the issue of whether those claims were valid.

The Trial

Some time in the year 30 A.D. Jesus seems to have decided to abandon his policy of concealment and to proclaim himself openly as the Messiah. His initial strategy of relying upon ethical teaching alone had not been an unqualified success. Matthew (11.20) records him as reproving Chorazin, Bethsaida and Capernaum as failing to respond adequately to his 'mighty works'; and in John 6.26 he tells the crowds 'Ye seek me, not because ye saw the miracles, but because ye did eat of the loaves'. Some seeds had fallen on stony ground, and neither miracles nor the Sermon on the Mount had produced any real change of heart in the mass of the population. Men were then much as they are today, when revivalist missions have only temporary effect. And if his own people, the Jews, had failed to give him a unanimous welcome, what better result might be expected by extending his mission to the surrounding nations? The only way forward was explicitly to claim authority as God's representative on earth.

However, the Messiah he was to reveal was neither a warrior nor a priestly Messiah, but a figure formed by study of passages in Isaiah and in other prophets. They are familiar to us from Handel's oratorio, *The Messiah*. This Messiah was to prevail through peaceful means. 'All shall be holy, and their king is the Lord Messiah. For he shall not put his trust in horse and rider and bow, nor shall he multiply unto himself gold and silver for war . . . For he shall smite the earth with the word of his mouth for evermore.' (Psalms of Solomon xlvii 35ff). The goal was the universal rule of God acknowledged by all men, when war, strife, and wickedness should cease; and to reach that goal it was required that Israel should become 'a kingdom of priests and a holy nation.'

Yet the possibility was envisaged that Israel might reject the call. 'He is despised and rejected of men; a man of sorrow and acquainted with grief . . . he was despised and we esteemed him not' (Isaiah 53.3). 'And one shall say unto him, "What are these wounds in thy hands?" Then shall he answer, "Those with which I was wounded in the house of my friends."' (Zech. 13.6).

Some texts even suggested a dishonoured death. 'He was oppressed, and he was afflicted, yet he opened not his mouth: he was brought as a lamb to the slaughter . . . He was taken out from prison and from judgement . . . for he was cut off out of the land of the living' (Is. 53.7 and 8).

But there could also be found a promise of resurrection. '(The Lord) hath smitten, and he will bind us up' (Hosea 6.1-2). 'For thou wilt not leave my soul in the grave; neither wilt thou suffer thy holy one to see corruption' (Psalm 16.10). 'God will redeem my soul from the grasp of the grave: for he shall redeem me' (Psalm 49.15).

After Jesus' death on the cross, his disciples diligently collected and assembled all these and other texts from Scripture to prove that he was indeed the Messiah and that everything had been foretold. And this conformity of fact with prophecy was not a complete accident. Jesus had himself deeply pondered these and similar passages to confirm the posture and attitude he intended to adopt. He had prepared for an ordeal, if that should come. There was still hope that his self-proclamation might inspire a full acceptance of himself and his message. But his premonitions were of rejection and death. So, Luke tells us, 'he steadfastly set his face to go to Jerusalem.'

Some scholars have contended that Jesus not merely foresaw but actively engineered and contrived his trial and crucifixion.

This is the theme of Schonfield: *The Passover Plot*,[1] taking up and expanding a similar suggestion by Hoskyns and Davey:

> Jesus acted as he did act and said what he did say because he was consciously fulfilling a necessity imposed upon him by God through the demands of the Old Testament. He died in Jerusalem, not because the Jews hounded him thither and did him to death, but because he was persuaded that, as Messiah, he must journey to Jerusalem in order to be rejected and to die.

The Riddle of the New Testament p. 160.

This is surely going too far. There is a difference between deliberate self-immolation and surrender to fate. And even that is a misnomer. For Fate is merely a metaphor for a combination of character with what, for convenience, we call chance. We come here upon the ancient dilemma for theists of how God can allow free will and yet foresee the future. Perhaps a comparison from the game of chess may assist. If a mere club player were pitted against the world champion, there would be no doubt about the final result; and yet this could be reached in a multitude of ways. At every move in the game, the club player would have complete freedom of choice. An infinity of variations and sub-variations would he open to him to select from. And yet his final defeat would he sure. It was, perhaps, part of God's plan for the world that Jesus should be condemned and crucified. But his fellow-countrymen, and especially the chief priests, were not bound to reject him. They were free agents, not manipulated puppets on a string. Nor was Jesus deliberately running upon his death. But he had no doubts of the hostility of the religious establishment towards him; and he was resolved to face the threat of death, if need be.

He was resolved to do so because some texts suggested that, resurrection or no, his death would be of measureless benefit to his people, a redeeming sacrifice to wipe away the guilt of all their sins. 'He was wounded for our transgressions, he was

bruised for our iniquities; and with his stripes we are healed . . .
Yet the Lord took thought for his tortured servant and healed
him who had made himself a sacrifice for sin' (Isaiah 53.5 and
10). His voluntary death could usher in a new age of hope, could
be a decisive turning point for better in the world.

In this belief he was not mistaken. No other event has had so
great an impact on history. And, ironically, his very non-
acceptance by the Jews was to gain for his message a wider and
more rapid dispersion. This is the theme of the early chapters of
the Book of the Acts. They tell of how persecution by the chief
priests had only the effect of spreading the Faith more widely, as
Jesus' followers fled abroad. Jesus' failure was his success.

We come accordingly to what scholars term the Passion
Narrative. As heard in performance, Bach's *St Matthew* or *St
John Passion* seem a plain and convincing tale. Yet almost every
detail and episode has been challenged and questioned by
learned scholars as unhistorical, and by none more rigorously
than Paul Winter.[2] He argues, generally, that Jesus was arrested
and put to death, not by the Jewish temple authorities, but by
the Romans. There never was any trial before the Sanhedrin;
for, if the high priests had wished to charge Jesus with
blasphemy, they had full power to pass and execute a sentence
of death by stoning. John (18.31) may represent the high priests
as claiming 'It is not lawful for us to put any man to death'; but
this is part of a Christian attempt to shift the blame for Jesus'
execution onto the Jews. It was vital to disguise the fact that he
had come to his end as a rebel against the Empire. But the
manner of his death betrays the truth: crucifixion was a purely
Roman mode of punishment. Pilate was not the fair-minded
and clement person the Gospels portray him as being, nor so
weak-minded as to seek an escape-hole in the *privilegium
Paschale* (the custom that one prisoner should be pardoned at
the Passover festival). That custom too is an evangelist's fiction.
Jesus was executed for the reason given on the *titulus* upon his

cross, for claiming to be the king of the Jews, for treason against Rome.

S.G. Brandon[3] takes this approach a step further. Winter still regards Jesus as having proclaimed the gospel of peace and as calling for denial of self. Brandon portrays him as a Zealot sympathiser and surrounded by Zealots committed to the violent overthrow of foreign domination. One follower, he points out, is specifically named as Simon the Zealot, and Jesus himself nicknamed James and John the Sons of Thunder. Then Judas' second name, Iscariot, suggests that he may have been one of the Sicarii. And Jesus' claim to be the Messiah was in itself treasonable, suggesting the illegitimacy of Rome's sovereignty. These facts about their origins were ones which the early Christians would be very anxious to hide, and especially so after the Jewish revolt of 66–70 A.D. Above all they needed to conceal the fact that their founder had been sentenced to death for sedition. Accordingly the accounts of his trial had to be written so as to throw the blame for his death upon the Jewish authorities. None of the evangelists states plainly that he was condemned by Pilate; and Mark's whole gospel, Brandon argues, is designed to portray mounting opposition from the lawyers and Pharisees that led finally to their condemnation of him in Council. The initiative is made to come, not from Pilate, but from the Jews.

Somehow too, Jesus had to be given a different image. Brandon[4] regards the Beatitudes ('Blessed are the peacemakers etc.') as a false attribution prompted by the Gentile Christians' policy of quietism. The 'gentle Jesus, meek and mild,' of the childhood prayer is a fiction. The real Jesus declared (Matt. 10.34) 'I came, not to send peace, but a sword.' Naturally Brandon regards the tale of Jesus' endorsement of the payment of tribute to Caesar as historically unfounded.

Brandon argues his thesis powerfully. But there are several items that it does not cover. The only really positive evidence is the names of a few of Jesus' followers; and here it is ambiguous. The Jewish historian[5] gives two dates for the emergence of the Sicarii: one in 6 A.D. and another in the years immediately preceding the Jewish rebellion of 66 A.D. So there can be no certainty that Judas Iscariot was one of them. And why should an extremist Zealot betray a Zealot sympathiser? The nickname 'Sons of Thunder' may just as easily have been coined to suit James' and John's hasty temperaments as their political inclinations. Their hotheadedness appears in Luke 9.54, when they ask that fire be poured down on a Samaritan village that failed to give Jesus adequate welcome. Again, why were Jesus' followers not arrested along with him? To accept Brandon's theory we have to write off, not merely the Beatitudes, but all the parables and many individual sayings.[6] Paul's letters must also be dismissed, since their ethical teaching reflects that of Jesus. Romans 12.17ff echoes the Sermon on the Mount.

Winter[7] regards even Jesus' triumphal entry into Jerusalem as of dubious historicity. As reported by Matthew, Jesus rode into the city on an ass so as to fulfil a prophecy in Zechariah (9.9): 'Tell the daughter of Zion, "Here is your king, who comes to you in gentleness, riding on an ass, riding on the foal of a beast of burden."' The objection has been made that this is a case of prophecy after the event. It cannot be that every Jew understood Zechariah's words as did Jesus' later followers; or no one would have dared ride a donkey in Jerusalem for fear of being thought to cherish Messianic ambitions! But in fact the ass was only part of the demonstration. Luke 19.37ff. makes clear that Jesus' followers (other Galileans, perhaps, as well as the twelve disciples) were also involved; and Mark (11.9) adds the detail that they had cut brushwood from the fields in readiness. It was not a case of Passover festival pilgrims waving the customary palm branches in spontaneous greeting.

To put all beyond doubt, his followers shouted 'Hosanna! Blessings on him who comes in the name of the Lord! Blessings on the coming kingdom of our father David!' Schonfield[8] notes that the words are the Hallel chant from Psalm 118.26. Some of the preceding verses imply a king going out to battle, and these would be a welcome on his victorious return.

Jesus' action was risky, and especially so at Passover time; for, whatever the earliest origins of that festival, it had come to be associated in Jewish folk memory with the people's escape from slavery in Egypt. It might have been called Liberation Day. Many Jews from the diaspora abroad would now have been visiting the city; and they would assume that any Messianic claimant would be one of the traditional, military type. The situation could easily have led to an anti-Roman riot. Nationalist feelings always ran high at this time; and the Romans, knowing this, took care to draft in extra troops. Alarmed at the prospect, some Pharisees begged Jesus to calm and rebuke his disciples.

However, there was no riot that day; or Jesus would surely have been arrested as the central figure. The Romans made no move. Perhaps they did not grasp the significance of the demonstration. They were accustomed to organised parties of pilgrims singing chants as they entered the Holy City, and may have assumed that this was just such another. Imperial policy had been, if possible, to maintain a low profile.

No riot ensued, and the day ended in what Winter regards as a suspicious anti-climax. Jesus left the city to spend the night in the nearby village of Bethany, in the house of Mary and Martha. What, after all, do people generally do after political and other demonstrations? They go home to bed. And Jesus was probably prudent enough not to stay in the city after dark, within range of the High Priest's troops. As John would put it, his hour had not yet come.

Next day, according to Mark (11.15ff.), 'he went into the temple and began driving out those who bought and sold in the temple. He upset the tables of the money-changers and the seats of the dealers in pigeons ... Then he began to teach them and said, 'Does not Scripture say, "My house shall be called a house of prayer for all the nations"? But you have made it a robbers' cave.'

This incident deserves a great deal of comment. Our first impression is that Jesus acted alone and in a burst of righteous indignation: he was appalled to see the way pilgrims were being exploited and holy ground put to improper, commercial use. Worshippers had to buy beasts and birds for sacrifice, and those destined for the purpose had to be officially certified as sound. The official tradesmen had a captive clientele. Moreover, only Palestinian coinage was acceptable – not any polluted with the Emperor's image; and dealing charges would be made for the transfer. We can guess, too, that fancy prices were demanded for victims for sacrifice. No doubt the pilgrims grumbled with each other afterwards in conversation, but still accepted the situation because of the convenience of the arrangements. They might have been pleased that someone was at last prepared to take bold action.

Yet this interpretation does not bear close scrutiny. Every conscientious Jew would visit the Temple at least every three years for the Passover; so that by the age of 30 Jesus would have had many opportunities to observe the scene. Had the abuse never affronted him before?

Brandon notes the difficulty and meets it with a plausible historical reconstruction. So far from Jesus' action being spontaneous and by him alone, he believes it to have been an organised coup. 'It is likely that it was achieved by the aid of an excited crowd of his supporters and was attended by violence and pillage.' (p. 333). No man, however dynamic his personality, could have succeeded in driving away from their place of business some legitimate traders when the Temple police were nearby to maintain order. 'Jesus was in effect attacking the sacerdotal aristocracy; for the money-changers and other traders could have operated there only under licence from the higher clergy who controlled the Temple (p. 331). This was a truly revolutionary act, for the High Priest held his office and authority from the Romans' (p. 332).

All this is very persuasive; and Brandon might point to Mark 11.16 ('he would not allow anyone to use the temple court as a thoroughfare for carrying goods')[9] as evidence that there was more than a temporary occupation. The difficulty is that, if we accept Jesus' ethical teaching as reported, such violent and direct action would have been quite out of character. We have to seek another explanation of Mark's very bald narrative.

This is not too difficult. It is a reasonable guess that Jesus had always found the practice of animal sacrifice as repulsive as we do today, and that he was further outraged by the blatant commercialisation that accompanied it; but, as a loyal Jew, he would have had grave inhibitions against taking any overt action against an established custom, and so would have hesitated long. Then, perhaps, his baptism experience may, as it were, have breached the psychological dam. But, if so, why wait until the last week of his life? These considerations suggest that John is right in placing the incident at an early stage in his ministry and on a previous visit to the city. This might, incidentally, explain why the lawyers and Pharisees were dogging his footsteps in Galilee, a remote area they would not normally visit.

As well as an instinctive revulsion against animal sacrifice, Jesus could have had more principled, theological objections to the practice. Feelings against it had been developing for five centuries among the more spiritually enlightened of his fellow-countrymen, and are expressed with particular force in the post-exilic Psalm 50:

> I am God, your God.
> Shall I not find fault with your sacrifices,
>   though your offerings are before me always?
> I need take no young bull from your house,
>   no he-goat from your folds. (vv. 7 and 8)

Jeremiah, writing about 600 B.C., expresses the same thought (7.22): 'When I brought your fathers out of Egypt, I gave no commands about whole-offering and sacrifice.'

It would be strange if Jesus did not share this antipathy.

Prof. Sanders[10] takes this thought a step further and links the Cleansing of the Temple with Jesus' prediction (Mark 13.1 ff.) of its destruction: 'You see these great buildings? Not one stone will be left upon another; all will be thrown down.' He believes that Jesus made his prophecy in such vehement tones that some bystanders thought that he was making a threat, and that this was accordingly made a charge against him in his trial; ('We heard him say, "I will pull down this temple, made with human hands, and in three days I will build another, not made with human hands."') Jesus' real meaning was that with the coming of the Kingdom of God there would be a new and perfect temple, built by God himself. His overturning of the money-changers' tables (perhaps only one or two) was purely a symbolic gesture to reinforce his words.[11] As we have seen (p. 75 above), Jesus was given to a dramatic style of utterance; and this fact is in favour of Prof. Sanders view.

The last words of the hostile witnesses' accusation, 'not made with hands', remind us of Jesus' interview with the Samaritan woman (John 4.19-25). She asks whether the proper place for worship is Mount Gerizim or Jerusalem, and is told that both places are to be superseded, and that real worshippers will worship the Father 'in spirit and in truth.' We may imagine Jesus saying much the same in Jerusalem. We can guess that the Cleansing provoked an immediate altercation with the Temple authorities, who would have accused him of an assault upon the national religion. In reply Jesus could have remarked *inter alia* that concentration upon the building and adornment of temples was an outdated conception of true religion, and indeed spiritually dangerous. 'Zeal for thy house will destroy me' (John 2.17).

Both Mark and John, after their accounts of the incident, go on to tell that the high priests and lawyers and elders asked Jesus for his authority for acting as he did. He is made to reply only with a counter-question: 'The baptism of John: was it from God, or from men?' – a question they preferred not to answer. This seems at first a shallow, debating tactic – until we reflect that the burden of the Baptist's message was that the Kingdom of God was at hand. In the new order of things Herod's temple would be a superfluity.

The rest of the week is filled up by Mark plausibly enough. The dispute with the high priests leads on naturally to the parable of the wicked tenants; and the testing question about the payment of tribute to Caesar could only have been asked in Judaea, which, unlike Galilee, was under direct Roman rule. It was shrewdly devised. Endorsement would have exposed Jesus to the charge of disloyalty to national aspirations, while a negative answer would have laid him open to an accusation of encouraging sedition. His reply, ('Render unto Caesar the things that are Caesar's, and to God the things that are God's') neatly evades the dilemma: so neatly and pithily that it is more probably Jesus' own rather than the invention of a later follower. It is a warning to churchmen not to be over concerned with political issues, or to try to sell religion by preaching politics: there is no short cut to evangelisation. The tale of the Widow's Mite also follows naturally; and so also does the clash with the aristocratic Saducees about the resurrection of the dead. They would not often have been found outside the capital.

Although Jesus' symbolic entry into Jerusalem did not provoke an anti-Roman demonstration, a disturbance soon followed. Barabbas (Mark 15.6) was arrested 'along with the rioters', and two *lestai* ('thieves' or 'trouble-makers'?) were crucified at the same time as Jesus. The Romans probably intimated that the Jewish authorities needed to keep better control of their own people, or they would lose some of their privileges. This is a threat reported by John (11.48) in an odd context. In his narrative it is Jesus' miracles, or 'signs' of his Messiahship that caused the Sanhedrin's alarm: 'If we leave him alone like this, the whole populace will believe in him. Then the Romans will come and sweep away our temple and our nation.' Caiaphas then declares, 'It is to your interest that one man should die for the people, and the whole nation not be destroyed.' This is to attribute to the High Priest and the Council an almost incredible lack of patriotism and religious faith. In the last war the men of Vichy handed over Resistance men to the Nazis; but that betrayal is barely comparable. No major figure was betrayed. In John's account the Jewish leaders are represented as proposing to hand over the central figure of Jewish faith. More probably Jesus' pungent criticisms of the religious establishment had convinced them that he was no more than a misguided trouble-maker and best got rid of. He had denigrated the exponents of the Holy Law, and so could not be genuinely inspired. Cooperation in his arrest would, therefore, both remove a troublesome personage and gain favour with Rome.

Arrangements were made accordingly; and we find in John 18.12 that the arrest was made by a unit of Roman soldiery under a Roman officer (*chiliarchos* being the Greek for military tribune). This detail definitely points to collusion between the High Priest and the Roman Governor. John is concerned throughout to present 'the Jews' as the villains of the piece, and would not have preserved the item unless genuinely historical. Another pointer to collaboration may be Pilate's early availability for the trial. But perhaps not too much should be made of this, as the Romans always rose early, scarcely breakfasted, and were mostly bearded rather than shaven.

The Last Supper probably took place at the house of 'the disciple whom Jesus loved' (John 13.23); and as host he was naturally reclining next to Jesus at the head of the table. Schonfield (p. 105) plausibly believes him to have been a young priest recruited during Jesus' earlier visit to Jerusalem. If so, there was no need of second sight for Jesus to know in advance of Judas' treachery. Moving, as he did, in Sanhedrin circles, he would have known of the plot and given timely warning.

It is a strange story. After Jesus' revelation of Judas' plan to betray him, the other disciples do not immediately seize him, but continue the meal as if nothing had occurred. This odd feature in the Gospel narratives was first pointed out by Enoch Powell in a letter to *The Times*[12] and reading it may have given Martin Scorsese a hint for his film, *The Last Temptation of Christ*. In it he represents Jesus as actually encouraging Judas to betray him so that he might be crucified in accordance with Scriptural prophecies. This is hard to believe, although it would fit in well with Schonfield's general thesis.

According to John 12.1-8, Jesus may have unintentionally given Judas a milder hint. When Mary anointed him with costly perfume, and Judas protested at the extravagance, Jesus defended her action, declaring she was merely beforehand in anointing his body for burial. If Judas was as mercenary-minded as the Gospels suggest, the words might have put the idea of selling his master into his head.

If, however, Jesus did not urge Judas' betrayal, he assuredly acquiesced in it. Otherwise he would not have tarried in the Garden of Gethsemane as he did. According to tradition he did so because he believed his coming execution to be God's will; and we have seen that there were Scriptural texts confirming that belief. His self-proclamation had not led to his unquestioned acceptance by the Jewish people. It remained to accept his alternative destiny.

Brandon theorises that there was no tarrying, and that Jesus and his followers were intercepted and attempted resistance. He makes much of Luke's mention of two swords (22.38) and of Peter's cutting off the servant of the High Priest's ear. But, if fighting really occurred, why was only Jesus arrested, and why, after his death, were his disciples allowed to go daily to the Temple? (Acts 5.42).

'They then led Jesus away to the High Priest's house, where the chief priests, elders and doctors of the law were all assembling' (Mark 14.53). A.N. Wilson[13] cannot have read the Gospels very carefully at this point; or he would not have written of the improbability of the members of the Sanhedrin having to be summoned from their beds and have urged this as a reason for regarding the ensuing trial as a mere fiction. According to Mark they had been alerted in advance and had never gone to bed, quite assured that Jesus would be intercepted on his way to Bethany by way of Gethsemane. The modern reader must choose between Mark's narrative and A.N. Wilson's conjecture.

Another piece of carelessness is A.N. Wilson's statement that Mark's narrative does not even claim to be based on eye-witness accounts (p. 213). He forgets that he had noted the existence among Jesus' friends of such members of the Sanhedrin as Nicodemus and Joseph of Arimathaea (p. 193). They would have been able to give a very full account of the proceedings at the trial.

Winter's reasons for doubting the historicity of what he calls Mark's Nocturnal Session are more substantial. He claims that, contrary to John 18.31 ('We are not allowed to put any man to death'), the Jewish authorities did indeed have the power of execution. Accordingly, if Jesus were being tried on purely religious grounds, the Sanhedrin could have proceeded on its own without reference to Pilate. Then, if convicted, Jesus would have been put to death by the traditional method of stoning. But in fact he was arrested and condemned as a rebel against Rome, and Mark's preliminary hearing would have been pointless.

Winter only partially proves his case. The strongest evidence in his favour is the case of Paul (Acts 21-26), who was arrested by a Roman officer for provoking an angry mob. It becomes clear that Paul did genuinely fear for his life if handed over by the Romans to a Jewish court. But it is also clear that the matter at issue was whether he had introduced a Gentile into the inner court of the Temple. The Jews' right to execute in such cases, the future emperor Titus reminded them, had been granted them only as a special privilege:[14] it was an example of Rome's tolerant and understanding administration. Clearly the case of Jesus was not parallel.

Other instances of stoning mentioned by Winter prove nothing. Stephen's martyrdom (Acts 7.54ff) was a case of a mob lynching rather than an orderly execution by the Jewish authorities. The rules for a stoning were very precise, and they were not followed on this occasion.[15] So Stephen's case is irrelevant. The only other major case known is the execution of Jesus' brother, James; and this too gives Winter no support. His stoning was a usurpation of procuratorial authority during the interregnum that followed the death of Festus.[16] How the military tribune Celer was executed is not clear. Because of his heinous conduct he was handed over to the Jews for punishment; but he was *sentenced* by the emperor Claudius.[17] Altogether the Jews seem not to have possessed jurisdiction in capital cases.

And this is what the study of Roman history would lead us to expect. Caesar regularly returned to his province in the non-campaigning winter months so as to conduct the assizes; and we read in Cicero and Pliny[18] of Roman governors acting as judges even in non-capital cases. The conduct of major law-suits normally lay with Rome; and very strong evidence is needed that this was not so in Judaea.

Winter's other arguments are less convincing. After narrating how Peter followed the soldiery at a prudent distance and then came into the High Priest's courtyard, Mark goes on to report Jesus' trial, and only then, when this is concluded, tells the tale of Peter's three denials of his master. Winter complains that the two actions could not have synchronized so neatly (p. 20ff): a regular trial would have long outlasted the taxing of Peter with his discipleship. All that must have occurred at Caiaphas' house was the making out of a charge sheet to take before Pilate.

But this is to ignore literary considerations. Mark uses a similar sandwich pattern in relating the incident of the Cleansing of the Temple (11.12-21), which he frames with Jesus' cursing of the barren fig tree and its withering. The effect is to lend both episodes greater emphasis. Similarly the postponement of Peter's final treachery till after Jesus' condemnation and the cock-crow adds greatly to its dramatic impact. It would have been poor literary craftsmanship to have interrupted the account of Jesus' trial with the story of the three challenges to Peter and his denials.

It has, finally, been argued that Mark's nocturnal session would have broken constitutional law and therefore could not have taken place.[19] But this is politically naive. Governments do act in this way. As recently as October 1992 the British Government encouraged the National Coal Board to contravene the law over the proposed closure of 31 pits. Schonfield (p. 147) plausibly suggests that the meeting was not a formal trial, but was convened in an attempt to find grounds for an accusation before Pilate.

Caiaphas needed this endorsement. No political or religious body is monolithic; and there are some indications that some members of the Sanhedrin might have questioned his action in cooperating in Jesus' arrest. Not all the Pharisees were of the nit-picking type portrayed in Mark's second chapter. Winter notes (p. 120) that some showed sympathy with the Christians as late as 62 A.D.; and we read in Acts 15.5 of the Pharisees becoming 'believers'. Luke (13.31-33) tells of some Pharisees warning Jesus that Herod Antipas was plotting against his life. Caiaphas was not securely in control of the Sanhedrin and was in fact later deposed.[20] He would not have dared to act alone. Rabbinic tradition was against the handing over of even one Jew as a scapegoat to a foreign nation;[21] and Jesus' was a critical case. Caiaphas had to show good and sufficient grounds for his arrest.

Finding material for a capital charge would, however, have been no easy task. In John 19.7 the chief priests accuse Jesus of claiming divinity for himself; but in fact he had never gone so far. His words to the paralytic, 'Your sins are forgiven you' (Mark 2.7), may imply that stance to the modern reader; but this is not necessarily so. Jews habitually avoided referring to God by name, and the words were a necessary circumlocution for 'God has forgiven you.' It may also be doubted whether Jesus was really at variance with the Jewish moral code in healing on the Sabbath (Mark 3.1-6). Prof. Vermes maintains that he was not, and goes on to argue more generally that Jesus was in line with liberal Jewish thought.[22] Nor would it have been easy to make good a charge of blasphemy. The rules governing such cases were exceedingly strict. The Torah required that the facts of the offence had to be agreed by two or more witnesses in exact detail. It would not have been sufficient to speak of Jesus' general attitude months before in his Galilean ministry. And in fact 'the witnesses did not agree' (Mark 14.57).

Apart from the one specific accusation that Jesus had threatened to destroy the Temple, Mark's account of the trial is vague and summary, with the result that scholars have found great difficulty in deciding, not only what the gravamen of the case against Jesus was, but why he should have been accused at all.

The most convincing recent work is that of Bowker, who carries a point made by Perrin a step further. Perrin argues that Jesus' welcoming attitude towards tax-gatherers had rendered him a traitor to the nation in Jewish eyes and effectively a Gentile. Bowker adds that all Pharisees would have been shocked by his over-lenient attitude towards repentant sinners[23] and to converts from the Gentile world. Both the liberal and conservative wings of Pharisaism looked on the Old Covenant as a two-way bargain between Yahweh and his people, whereby God would act in his benevolence only if Man made at least a sincere attempt to carry out the provisions of the Torah and the oral tradition. The liberal Hillel and his school did not expect the convert to observe every jot and tittle of the Law at once; but in the end he must fully conform. They required an earnest of his future rectitude. Jesus, however, demanded no more than an initial declaration of faith.

Jesus might also have been accused of theological presumption. The Pharisees rested their pronouncements upon quotation from precedents and tradition, building carefully upon the legal interpretations of scribe after scribe. Jesus taught 'with authority and not as the scribes'. The clearest example of the difference comes in what are known as the Six Antitheses in the Sermon on the Mount (Matt. 5.21). 'Ye have heard that it was said by them of old time, Thou shalt not kill . . . But I say unto you, That whosoever is angry with his brother without cause shall be in danger of the judgment.' A. Ginzberg[24] regards this language as a mark of overweening arrogance. 'Israel cannot accept as religious, as the Word of God, the utterances of a man who speaks in his own name – not 'thus saith the Lord', but 'I say unto you'. This 'I' is in itself enough to drive Judaism from the Gospels for ever.' The Six Antitheses are not in their content a frontal attack on the Law of Moses. But their manner of expression was novel and challenging.

These last two points may have been somewhat above the heads of ordinary folk. What was not was Jesus' welcoming attitude towards the Samaritans. Relations between them and the Jews had been particularly strained since the Samaritans' defilement of the Temple during the festival of Passover between 6 and 9 A.D.[25] Any public figure speaking well of them would have risked unpopularity. But in the Gospels they are given an almost defiantly good press. The parable of the good Samaritan (Luke 10.29ff.) is an obvious example. Another is that of the

Samaritan who, alone of ten lepers, had the grace to return and express thanks for his cure (Luke 17.16). In John 8.48 Jesus himself is accused of having Samaritan blood in him. It is as if a member of Sinn Fein were charged with being a Protestant, or an Israeli with being half-Arab. The taunt says much about Jesus' reputation.

Jesus may well have been unpopular on these counts. But they were not material for a criminal prosecution; and the case against him seems to have been breaking down. At last, putting him on oath, the high Priest asked him the direct question, 'Are you the Messiah?' According to Mark, Jesus simply answered 'Yes'. According to Matthew he replied 'You have said (that)' (*su eipas*). Some scholars, including Prof. Vermes, regard this as an ambiguous reply, which Mark took as an affirmative. But it is improbable that, having proclaimed his Messiahship by the manner of his entry into Jerusalem, Jesus would now have sought to disown that status. The words must have had the tone of the American 'You've said it'.

This would have been taken by the Roman authorities as a declaration of rebellious intent; but no patriotic Jew could have greeted the revelation with anything but pleasure. The only objection could have been that Jesus should not have presumed to make the claim himself. J.C. O'Neill[26] theorises that a Messianic claimant had to await God's announcement of his identity, and that Jesus had failed to do this. But Jesus could surely argue that God had given sufficient 'signs' (to use John's term) in the miracles of healing Jesus had been given power to perform. These clearly indicated his status.

To be the Messiah was the very opposite of a crime. However, Jesus went on gratuitously to make a much larger claim: 'and you will see the Son of Man (i.e. me) seated at the right hand of God and coming with the clouds of heaven.' Quotation from the book of Daniel or no, this could only be an assertion of divine status; and this, in Jewish eyes, was a blasphemy. Jesus had condemned himself for the Sanhedrin out of his own mouth. The doubters in the assembly were won over; and they began to offer him violence.

On then, in the early morning, to Pilate; a man of whom our contemporary Jewish sources tell us little good. Former governors had tactfully kept the legionary standards draped; for on them was the image of the reigning emperor, a blasphemy in Jewish eyes. Pilate provocatively conveyed them to Jerusalem unsheathed, Josephus[27] tells us. Another witness is Philo, in his account of the Jewish embassy to the emperor Gaius. He describes Pilate as a man of inflexible disposition, harsh, and obdurate,[28] and goes on to tell how in Tiberius' reign Pilate feared that Jewish notables would send a delegation to the Emperor exposing his arbitrary government, including executions without trial. Luke (13.1) tells that he mingled the blood of Galileans with their sacrifices – with what provocation we cannot know. The evidence of Josephus and Philo is not impartial, but is enough to suggest that Pilate would not go out of his way to be obliging or merciful. Yet the Gospels represent him as fair-minded, though lacking in determination. The Aramaic *Toledoth Jesu*[29] too tells of Pilate favouring Jesus against his accusers. What is the explanation?

The simplest lies in Jesus' own demeanour. Expecting a Che Guavara Pilate was non-plussed to find standing before him a Mahatma Ghandi. Accustomed to dealing with shifty criminals he suddenly found himself confronted with a man transparently honest and upright. The main accusation would not have been consonant with the appearance and stance of the prisoner before him. In the circumstances, Pilate's natural reaction would have been to seek further evidence. And this, according to Luke's gospel, is precisely what he did.

Whereas Mark speaks vaguely of 'many charges', Luke writes that Jesus was accused of spreading disaffection, starting with his own native area of Galilee. 'When he heard this, Pilate asked if the man was a Galilean, and on learning that he belonged to Herod's jurisdiction he remitted the case to him; for Herod was also in Jerusalem at that time.' (Luke 23.6,7).

The main charge now was no longer blasphemy, but the claim to be the Messiah, and so a threat to existing rulers (including Herod). Hence the mimicry of sending Jesus back to Pilate dressed in a gorgeous robe. 'The same day Pilate and Herod became friends: till then there had been a standing feud between them.' Schonfield[30] conjectures that the bad feeling between them had arisen when Pilate proposed to divert the sacred funds for the construction of an aqueduct, and when Roman troops killed many Galileans partaking in a demonstration of protest.

According to the Gospels, Jesus broke silence before Pilate only over the one charge of being the Messiah, and in John 18.36 he explains that his kingdom is not of this world and that he is called to witness to the truth. Should we rather write Truth with an initial capital? (The Greek language reserves them for proper names; so that its absence from the text is no argument against this suggestion.) It would be natural for it to be found as a key word in the *Gospel of Thomas*; but it is not. However, the words are reminiscent of John 14.6 ('I am the way, the truth, the life'); and there are several suggestive examples in the Old Testament, e.g. Psalm 100.5: 'his (God's) truth endureth from generation to generation' and Ps. 119.142: 'thy law is the truth' (vide also Ps. 15.2 and John 16.13). It would not be surprising to find it as a pivotal term, not only in Johannine, but also in Jesus' own theology. Clearly there were only Romans present at the interrogation, so that we cannot be certain of what passed; but it is credible enough that Jesus used the words attributed to him by John. Pilate's counter-question, 'What is Truth?', was probably uttered with smiling irony, as if to ask 'And what is this great mystery?'

Why did Jesus maintain silence in all his trials? Schonfield[31] suggests that he did so so as to fulfil a prophecy in Isaiah, 'As a sheep before her shearers is dumb . . .' (53.7). A more plausible theory is that Mark, having no actual record of the trials, invented this detail. But as we have seen, there *were* potential witnesses and informants. We should reflect that some of the charges, those of blasphemy and of stirring up disaffection for instance, were not easy for Jesus to dissipate single-handed, and that the burden of proof would have lain with his accusers. He did best to remain silent.

Apparently Pilate did not proceed any further with his examination, but reminded the Jews that there was a custom for the governor to release one prisoner for them at Passover, and offered them a choice of Jesus or another. Winter[32] declares that this *privilegium paschale* is a mere invention of Christian propagandists, urging that there is no reference to its existence in Jewish sources. But this argument from silence is notoriously weak, and it is highly unlikely that the evangelists should have invented a practice so strikingly peculiar.

Another of Winter's suggestions[33] is much more convincing. He points out that as late as the 10th century old codices were circulating in which Barabbas' name was written 'Jesus ho Barabbas', and concludes that the name meant 'Jesus, son of the Rabbi', (just as Simon Bar Jonah in Matt 16.17 means 'Simon, son of Jonah'). Moreover, John's 'Now Barabbas was a robber' is probably an unjustified inference from Mark's account, where Barabbas is arrested 'along with the rioters'. Again, Matthew's description of him as *episemos* (27.16) could just as easily mean 'distinguished' as 'notorious' (Similarly the English 'egregious' had once both a complimentary and pejorative sense according to context.) All this points to Barabbas as having been a respectable person caught up in a melée; and we can conclude that Pilate regarded both Jesus 'called Christ' and Jesus Barabbas as doubtful cases among those brought before him for seditious and lawless behaviour, and, rather favouring 'Jesus called Christ' of the two, mentioned the *privilegium paschale* as a justification for his release. The High Priest and his followers opted for the mercy to be extended to Barabbas.

Pilate now had Jesus flogged and proposed this as a sufficient punishment; but the High Priest and his party insisted upon crucifixion. 'If you let this man go, you are no friend to Caesar.' These words were decisive. For this was the period of a reign of terror in Rome, when prominent men fell victims to the suspicions of the emperor Tiberius. Tacitus has overdrawn the picture; but no provincial governor could face a complaint of misgovernment with equanimity; and the Jews had already succeeded in disposing of one ruler in the person of Archelaus. They had realised their power, and might appeal to Caesar once again. Pilate preferred not to take the risk, and ordered Jesus' crucifixion. The High Priest had his will, and Jesus was sentenced to the cross as a rebel against Rome.

We need not follow the grisly details except for two points. Crucifixion was devised as a lingering death of prolonged agony lasting more than a day. Yet Jesus was dead by three in the afternoon, reports Mark. Winter[34] explains that a preliminary scourging was a regular part of the penalty of crucifixion and was often so severe as to inflict mortal wounds, crucifixion itself merely prolonging the condemned man's ordeal. This must have been the case with Jesus, who was so weakened as to be unable to carry his own cross. Schonfield conjectures that Jesus had deliberately planned a sham death so that he could be taken down from the cross by his followers and revived. The means was to be a drug administered to him in a wine-soaked sponge. He points out that Josephus records cases of men being pardoned and surviving crucifixion. The hypothesis fits the evidence well except in one respect. We cannot suppose that Jesus imagined that he could make an atoning sacrifice for his people by means of a fiction and a charade. Winter's explanation is to be preferred.

Just before his death Jesus cried aloud, 'My God, my God, why hast thou forsaken me?' We might have expected Christian apologists to have suppressed this utterance, which sceptics have seized on as evidence that Jesus was a deluded madman awakened to reality at last. It so happens that the words are also the first verse of the 22nd psalm, and it has been suggested that Jesus was reciting this as appropriate to his situation. But this is no more credible than that a prisoner upon the rack should divert himself with a passage from Shakespeare. It is simplest to regard them as evidence of the evangelist's determination to give the world a true and unvarnished record.

RESURRECTION?

'The Resurrection is something very difficult to believe in; and something even more difficult not to believe in', a former school chaplain once remarked.

This puts the Christian case in a nutshell. We think instinctively that such an event cannot have occurred; and so we believe *a priori* that the reports of the phenomenon are incredible. They contradict all the known facts of experience and are at variance with all the findings of modern science. The burden of proof is, therefore, altogether on those who maintain the truth of the Biblical accounts. And, when we come to look closely at these, we find that they are not entirely consistent with one another. The Synoptic Gospels are no longer synoptic. It is no longer a case of Matthew and Luke following Mark with additions of their own. We are dealing now with four independent testimonies, which, on the face of it, do not seem quite to square with each other. To see how important these discrepancies are, it is best to reconstruct, so far as we can, an account of the occurrences alleged in chronological order, and to pass comment as we proceed.

1) After obtaining permission from Pilate, Joseph of Arimathaea deposits Jesus' body in a rocky tomb, which he closes with a rolling stone. Mary Magdalene and Mary, mother of Joseph, watch the process (*Mark* 15.47). *Matthew* (27.55f) concurs.

2) Next day (the Sabbath) the chief priests and Pharisees

come in a body to Pilate and ask that a guard be put over the tomb. 'That impostor' had predicted that he was to be raised from death after three days, and their fear is that his disciples may secretly remove the body so as to give the impression that the prophecy has been fulfilled (*Matthew alone*). Pilate agrees, and a guard is accordingly stationed; but whether of Roman soldiers or of the Temple police is not clear. The Greek text might mean either 'Have your guard!, or You have a guard'.

The tale implies that Jesus did indeed predict his own resurrection. Instances of his doing so have been dismissed by some scholars as prophecies after the event concocted by the evangelists; but, in that case, there would have been no need or justification for a guard over the tomb. The reports of this and of Jesus' prophecies are interdependent. We cannot credit the former and not the latter.

3) Early on the third day, just after sunrise (*Mark*), some of Jesus' women followers come to the tomb to anoint his dead body. In *Mark* there are three: Mary Magdalene, Mary mother of James, and Salome. *Matthew* speaks only of two: Mary Magdalene and 'the other Mary' (presumably Mary, the mother of James and Joseph, whom he has recorded as watching the entombment). But among those he lists as watching the Crucifixion is the mother of the sons of Zebedee (27.56), instead of Salome as given by Mark (15.40). This suggests that the two are the same person and that Matthew may merely have omitted to mention her on this occasion. *Luke* names the women as Mary Magdalene, Mary the mother of James, and Joanna, 'who had accompanied Jesus from Galilee.' *John* has only Mary Magdalene visiting the tomb early, while it is still dark; but he later has her saying 'We do not know where they have laid him', implying that there were others with her.

So, so far as the women's names are concerned, there is a rough agreement in the sources. It should also be noted that, contrary to the sceptical Kirsopp Lake's theory, they should not have come to the wrong tomb, since two at least of them had watched the entombment.

They find the stone rolled back.

4) The women enter the tomb and find a young man wearing a white robe (*Mark*), two men in dazzling garments (*Luke*), an angel (*Matthew*), who had previously rolled the stone away, (the guards meanwhile lying dazed) and who was now sitting on it (Matt. 28.1-4). Mark has the man sitting, and Luke the men standing.

We have to consider whether these variations are material or are due simply to the women's startled and nervous state of mind. In appearance Matthew's angel might have looked much like Mark's young man. Angels acquire wings only in later religious art, to distinguish them from the human characters. In Jacob's dream they have need of a ladder to ascend from earth to heaven, and in their visit to Abraham in Genesis 18 they are mistaken for men. The Greek word *angelos* means merely 'messenger', and delivering a message is what Matthew's angel does – a message that is the same in substance as that of Mark's young man. But Matthew's angel is also credited with rolling away the stone after a violent earthquake. In *John* we find a different explanation of the stone's displacement put into the mouth of Mary Magdalene. 'They have taken the Lord out of his tomb' she tells Peter and 'the other disciple'. Who can 'they' be? The only persons she could have meant are the guard. But her conclusion is almost certainly wrong; for, if the High Priest and his servants had done such a thing, they had only to produce the dead body in order to disprove tales of Jesus' resurrection. And they did not. The words do, however, suggest that Matthew's story of a guard being set is no fiction.

Could the disciples have removed the body by stealth? Hardly. Not all the guard would have been on watch at once. Most would have been at rest after posting a single sentry with instructions to turn them out on any unusual development. And sentries have been known to sleep at their posts. But not, surely, while a great boulder is being manhandled; and, as we shall shortly find, most of the disciples were not now in Jerusalem. Prof. Vermes regards the rumour that the disciples stole the body as improbable, but is satisfied that the tomb was indeed empty.

Who, then, *did* move the stone? Schonfield's solution is the young man who administered a drug to Jesus while still on the cross. As a chief plotter, he would then have removed the stone, taken Jesus away for revival, and then returned to play the part of Mark's young man — a very active participant. This would be a neat solution to the problem if we could accept Schonfield's main thesis. But, as we have seen (p. 108 above), that overstrains belief. If Jesus had been such a charlatan as Schonfield imagines, he would never have delivered the Sermon on the Mount or composed the parables.

We are forced back to Matthew's angel and earthquake. And the first should not be too easily rationalised away. If we are prepared to accept as a hypothesis the possibility of Jesus' resurrection, then we ought also be prepared to accept that there may be such beings as angels. If we accept the possibility of the supernatural in the one instance, we should in logic accept it also in the other. We should not swallow a camel and then gag over a gnat. And, if we do not believe in Matthew's angel, we have to make some plausible guess as to the identity of the alternative person of Mark's young man. It is not easy to find a candidate.

The earthquake might be merely the typical stage accompaniment of the supernatural in a Biblical narrative, but may also have been the motive force of the stone's dislodgement. Clearly some loud noise awoke the main guard, who would then have inspected the open tomb, found it empty, and sped off in alarm to the chief priests to report the situation.

5) The women are told that Jesus has been raised from the dead as predicted and (*only in Mark and Matthew*) that they are to

tell the disciples that he 'goeth before you (*proagei*) into Galilee' and 'you will see him there.' Some scholars take *proagei* as a prophetic present tense and translate: 'intends to conduct you.'

6) The women then return and report the news to the Eleven and all the others (Luke); run off in awe and great joy to tell the disciples (*Matthew*); run off, beside themselves with terror, and say nothing to anybody (*Mark*). Here the oldest and most reliable of Markan manuscripts ends. According to *John* (20.2) Mary Magdalene (the youngest and most agile?) runs off to inform Peter and 'the other disciple, the one whom Jesus loved.'

Why inform only these two? Is the explanation that they were the only ones who stayed in the city during the trial, while the rest fled to Bethany and were still there? If so, there is a conflict in our sources, since Luke implies that all were now in the city. This is unlikely. When Jesus was arrested in the garden of Gethsemane, lying to the east of the city, most of his disciples fled; and they would most naturally have made for Bethany, another mile or so to the south-east, where Jesus regularly retired for the night, away from the Temple guards. Bethany, we remember, was the home of Martha and Mary. As Jews they could not have come back to, say, the house of the Last Supper on the day after the Crucifixion, since that would have involved more than a Sabbath day's journey (about 1000 yards). Then, next day they could hardly have made the journey before the women set out for the tomb. The only way to save Luke's credit is to assume that he carelessly altered a source which read, like Matthew, 'to tell the disciples' to '(in fact) reported all this' and, for good measure, called 'the disciples', 'the Eleven and all the rest.' John is the most accurate at this point.

7) According to *Matthew* the women are met on their way back by Jesus, who repeats the angel's/young man's instructions. We have, perhaps, to guess that these were the two older and slower women.

8) Peter and the other disciple run to the tomb (*John*). The

latter arrives first, but 'went not in.' This fits in with the conjecture that he was a young priest, and therefore observed the religious taboo on contact with the dead. They see the linen grave clothes lying discarded and conclude that Jesus has been resurrected. They do not see Jesus.

9) According to *John*, Mary Magdalene must also, but later, have returned to the tomb, where she seems to be alone. She peers into the tomb and sees two angels (the same as Luke's two men in dazzling garments?), who ask her why she is weeping. Turning back she sees Jesus, but takes him for the gardener.

There is a peculiarity here that needs explanation. The two disciples on the road to Emmaus (see 11 below) also fail to recognise the risen Jesus. This suggests that we are not dealing with hallucinations. In that case familiar figures would have their known features. Also worthy of comment is the way in which she offers to embrace the risen Jesus but is checked by him with the explanation that he has not yet returned to his Father. This is an incident that only the most imaginative fiction writer would invent.

10) According to *Luke*, the women had previously 'reported all this to the Eleven and all the others' – as we have seen, probably a false inference. In Luke 24.12 Peter runs to the tomb to check up on the women's story: but this sentence is not found in the earliest manuscript and looks like an addition to the text to make it square with John's account.

11) Still on the Sunday, the risen Jesus walks and talks with two of 'the others' on the road to Emmaus (*only in Luke*). This is probably the modern Kaloniyeh, four or five miles to the west of Jerusalem. An Emmaus at this distance is mentioned by Josephus and suits the story better than any place twice the distance, as in Luke. One of them is named Cleopas and may be the husband of the mother of James and John ('the other Mary'). They speak of the women's having had a vision of angels (no longer the 'two men'). Sceptics may suggest that the incident is a

doctrinal pericope with the punchline: 'He was known to them at the breaking of the bread'.

12) They return from Emmaus late on Sunday evening (*Luke*) to be told that the Lord has appeared unto Simon (Peter). They find the Eleven and the rest assembled.

Jesus then appears to the whole company, instructing them to preach the Gospel to all nations, beginning at Jerusalem. According to *John* (20.24) Thomas was not with the rest, but he agrees (20.19) that this appearance did occur 'late that Sunday evening'.

13) A week later, (*John*) in response to Thomas' doubts, Jesus appears and calls on him to inspect the marks of the nails in his hands and the hole in his side. The language of the concluding words suggests that this passage was read aloud separately and used for teaching purposes. An accurate translation would run, 'Happy are the kind of people who did not see me (*hoi me idontes* is the equivalent of a generic relative clause) and yet made an act of belief' (*pisteusantes*: instantaneous aorist). The words can refer to future converts and point a moral.

However, that Thomas was personally convinced of Jesus' resurrection cannot be doubted; for when the Portuguese landed on the Malabar coast in 1501 A.D., they found there a long-established and orthodox Christian community that claimed him as their founder. This is a piece of evidence similar to the discovery of Peter's tomb below St Peter's, Rome. It is evidence about our evidence.

14) Jesus leads the disciples out to Bethany and then parts from them. They return to Jerusalem (*Luke*).

15) There is a conflict here between Luke and *Matthew*, who has the Eleven make their way to a mountain in Galilee (some distance from Bethany), from where Jesus' ascension takes place. In the absence of the parallel ending to Mark's gospel, now lost, this looks like a mere extrapolation from the instructions given to the women at the tomb. It is at this point that the

discrepancies between the Gospels become most serious. The author of *Acts* (also Luke?) reports the Ascension as taking place from Mount Olivet, which *is* not far from Bethany.

16) *John* records another resurrection appearance by the Lake of Tiberias. But this seems to be a later addition to his gospel, perhaps by another hand. The conclusion to the work had already been written in the previous chapter (20.30f):

> There were indeed many other signs that Jesus performed in the presence of his disciples, which are not recorded in this book. Those here written have been recorded in order that you may hold the faith that Jesus is the Christ, the Son of God ...

There is a further difficulty about the passage. According to John 20.22 the disciples had been given the charge to spread the Gospel. Yet here Peter goes off fishing as if he had never met Jesus. The passage ends with the charge to Peter to 'feed my sheep', i.e. to become Pope; and this mission is symbolised by the number of fishes (153) caught in the net. Ancient zoology regarded 153 as the total number of different species; and this fact gives us the clue to the meaning. Peter is being represented as a fisher of men, and an extremely successful one, destined to bring in every nation in his haul. The chapter heralds the primacy of the see of Rome.

These are the only specific post-resurrection appearances of Jesus recorded in the Gospels. To them the author of Acts adds an indefinite number occurring in the forty days following the first Sunday, during which he taught the disciples about the Kingdom of God. There seems to have been need of this training. They asked whether he would now restore the kingdom to Israel. In other word they were still viewing him as a national Messiah and liberator rather than as the universal saviour of all mankind. They really were 'slow to understand'. If our author is correct, Jesus' mission was still far from being accomplished. A number of parables had not made full impact.

This lack of understanding among the disciples and the priority given to their further instruction is very hard to credit. Yet otherwise, unless the time were occupied in this way, there is a surprising delay in their making the fact of Jesus' resurrection public knowledge. They apparently did not do so until the feast of Pentecost, some seven weeks later. They would naturally have been thought eager to tell the whole world of the event. And this rather long interval between the Resurrection and its proclamation is also a difficulty for those who theorise that the phenomenon was a purely psychological event, that the real miracle was, not Jesus' actual reappearance, but the disciples' new-found confidence and sense that the Lord was with them. In that case this overwhelming spiritual experience, which they felt impelled to communicate to all, was somewhat slow in coming.

The excuse might be made that Jesus' followers needed time in which to pluck up their courage, that they feared for their physical safety. But, as we have seen, no attempt was made to arrest anyone except Jesus himself, and we are told (Acts 2.46) that they openly visited the Temple every day. Initially they were unmolested, even after Peter's Pentecost day address to the crowds. It was only after the new movement began to show signs of success that the chief priests issued a warning against preaching in the Name. Actual persecution did not begin until after Stephen's martyrdom. And here we should, perhaps, note that he had made greater claims for Jesus than had Peter. Peter had still referred to Jesus as 'a man' (Acts 2.22), although an exceptional man and the Messiah, whose status had been confirmed by his resurrection. Stephen (Acts 7.56) ascribes to him divine status. The Temple authorities now felt that they were dealing with a much greater heresy than they had first imagined.

Saul (later named Paul) 'was consenting to his (Stephen's) death', and soon became one of the chief persecutors of the new sect. Which brings us to the fact that sceptics and unbelievers also have some explaining to do. They have to account, first of all, for two unexpected conversions to Christianity: those of Paul and Jesus' brother, James. That of Paul is more easily understood than might appear.

We have to remember that ideological antagonists are always more familiar with their opponents' doctrines than are the general public. I recollect from my student days how, despite their wrongheaded advocacy of our making a 'People's Peace' with Hitler, I could still feel a certain respect for the Communists. Even though their proposed policies were simplistic, the Marxist diagnosis of the failures of capitalism had much truth in it. And they were idealists: their hearts were in the right place. Some, like Burgess and Maclean, came from well-to-do families, and were sincere enough to volunteer for service in the Spanish civil war. John Cornford died there. So, if I had suddenly swopped party allegiance, reasons could have been found. Similar thought processes account for the way some Communists switched to becoming the Party's determined and violent foes. Arthur Koestler (himself an ex-Communist) noted how some, upon their recantation, would urge as decisive considerations the very arguments that they had previously derided.[1] Alone in private these had had their impact.

Paul's conversion is very largely parallel. He was 'a Pharisee among the Pharisees', some at least of whom were sympathetic to Jesus and warned him that Herod Antipas was his foe. He would have believed in the resurrection of the dead, though not until the Last Day. And he might well have admired Stephen's demeanour even while voting for his death. The springs of Christianity could have been welling up within him unseen.

The parallel is not, however, quite precise. Politics, with its sub-division of economics, is not an exact science, but a matter of choosing the better of various courses of action, none of which can guarantee success. For Paul, faced with the challenge of Christianity, the issue was one, not of conduct or action, but of fact. Did he, or did he not, believe that the voice that spoke to him on the Damascus road was that of the risen Christ? Twenty centuries later we can only observe that his ensuing temporary blindness could have been the result of a nervous shock, and that from then on Paul always spoke of Jesus' resurrection as an assured fact.

The other instance of a surprising conversion to Christianity is one that a hasty reader might think no surprise at all, and indeed unnecessary – that of Jesus' brother James. One might think Jesus' own family would have supported him from the first. But the opposite was the case. Very early in his career his relatives came to take charge of him, declaring that he was out of his mind (Mark 3.21); and in Matthew (13.57) we find him complaining, 'A prophet will always be held in honour, except in his home town, and in his own family:' The blasphemous import of these passages is such that we cannot believe that the evangelists invented the incidents. The typical propagandist would have suppressed such reports. Initially at least Jesus had to face disbelief and opposition from his own kith and kin. Yet in the book of Acts we find James as head of the Jerusalem church, with greater authority than Peter. What changed his attitude?

A plausible explanation would be that James' doubts were overcome by Jesus' series of miraculous cures and exorcisms. But, if we can trust Mark's order of events, some of these preceded his family's scepticism. Some writers have maintained that the decisive factor was Jesus' resurrection appearance to James recorded in Paul's first letter to the Corinthians (15.3). This document is commonly dated to 52 A.D. (or a mere twenty odd years after the Crucifixion), and is accordingly the earliest extant account of the resurrection appearances. So it is worth quoting in full:

> I handed on to you the facts that had been imparted to me: . . .
> that he (Christ) was raised to life on the third day, according to
> the scriptures; and that he appeared to Cephas, and afterwards to

the Twelve. Then he appeared to over five hundred of our brothers at once, most of whom are still alive, though some have died. Then he appeared to James, and afterwards to all the apostles. In the end he appeared to me.

The same appearance is reported in a surviving fragment of the lost *Gospel of the Hebrews*, but with details that indicate that it was not this event which prompted James' conversion, but that he had already come to believe in Jesus and his mission before his trial. It reads as follows:

> But the Lord, when he had given the *sindon* to the high priest's servant, went to James and appeared to him. For James had sworn that he would not eat bread from that hour when he had drunk the Lord's cup until he saw him rising from those who sleep ... 'Bring,' says the Lord, 'a table and bread.' He took bread and blessed it and broke it and gave it to James the Righteous and said to him, 'My brother eat your bread, for the Son of Man has risen from those who sleep.'[2]

This portrays James as one of the guests at the Last Supper, and so convinced of his brother's future resurrection that he took an oath to abstain from food until this had occurred. It is the kind of detail that might have been penned by a Jewish Christian writer eager to emphasise the loyal saintliness of the head of his own church; but it is of dubious historicity. It is hard to believe that James had foreknowledge both of the result of Jesus' trial and execution, let alone of his resurrection. It is clear that there was something in Jesus that prevailed over his family's original scepticism; but whether James was won over before or by Jesus' resurrection cannot be proved from this passage.

However, the most remarkable assertion in this fragment is that Jesus' first resurrected appearance was not to one of his close adherents, but to the servant of the High Priest (the same whose ear Peter had cut off (Luke 22.51)?) The *sindon* referred to must be the linen burial shroud, which John tells us was to be seen

121

lying in the empty tomb. Was the High Priest's servant, then, instructed to return this to the tomb and to inform the women visitors that Jesus had arisen and would go before his disciples into Galilee? Was he Mark's young man that they found sitting in the tomb? The conjecture seems fantastic. It is easier to believe in Matthew's angel. Perhaps it is part of a general Judaising colouring of the work and reflects a tendency in the Judaean Christians to appease the Temple authorities.

We have so far been dealing with positive evidences for Jesus' resurrection. There is also some important negative evidence. Sceptics have to explain why Jesus' crucifixion was not the end of him and his movement. For there were other Messianic claimants in these years, who have largely disappeared from history. Two of them are mentioned in the New Testament. Theudas (Acts 5.36) boasted to 'be somebody' and is described by Josephus[3] as a *goes*, 'a sorceror, cheat', who claimed to be a prophet. He persuaded a number of Jews to follow him to the River Jordan, which he promised to divide miraculously. He failed, was captured, and beheaded.

Another was the Egyptian Jew who led four thousand terrorists out into the wilds (Acts 21.36). We learn from Josephus the additional information that he assembled a following on the Mount of Olives and promised that the walls of Jerusalem would fall at his command. They did not, and he also was suppressed.

Besides these aspirant Messiahs, Brandon has assembled a number of others, known only to historians of Judaism. The pro-Roman Josephus tends to describe all of them as 'bandits', just as the Ian Smith regime in Rhodesia christened all the followers of Mugabe and Nkomo 'terrorists'. (Often in history the choice of words between 'bandit' and 'freedom-fighter' depends on which side has the writer's sympathy.) Rather significantly, most came from one family; for political allegiances tend to be hereditary. (One thinks easily of the Pitts, the Asquiths, and the Salisburys.)

The best known is Judas the Galilean, who raised revolt at the time of the Census and the land-tax that it foreshadowed. The land was God's, he claimed, and Roman rack-renting a sacrilege. The Jews should have no king but God. His appeal to force failed, and he paid the penalty with his life.

His father, Hezekiah, had similar aspirations, but was defeated and slain by Herod the King. Josephus calls him a brigand, but he was clearly something more; for Herod was called before the Sanhedrin to justify his action.

Two of Judas' sons continued the tradition of resistance and were crucified by the procurator Tiberius Alexander about 46 A.D., and another son was the Menahem who headed the great rebellion of 66 A.D. He came to Jerusalem and assumed the leadership of it as the rightful king and probably, thinks Brandon, as the Messiah. When Jerusalem had fallen, the Zealots made a last stand at Masada under Eleazar, another relative.[4]

All these other would-be Messiahs had their claims punctured by Roman swords or nails. And that was that. No one ever claimed that Menahem's tomb was empty, or of having seen Judas the Galilean after his death. Their names are known only to specialist historians. But Jesus' name is known world wide. This is a difference which sceptics have to explain. On the positive side they have also to explain the rise of Christianity.

This is a case of 'That which is nearest the eye the eye cannot see.' We are so used to describing members of the Faith as Christians and to hearing 'Jesus' and 'Christ' as alternative names that we do not sufficiently inquire as to how this came about.

For the Gentile world it was through a very roundabout process. 'Christ' is merely the Greek equivalent of 'the Messiah'; and the disciples would have had to begin by explaining this Jewish conception: that the Messiah was the Jews' hoped for national liberator,[5] who would 'restore the kingdom to Israel' and bring all nations under his sway, himself ruling under God. He was, in Field Marshal Montgomery's phrase, to knock the surrounding nations for six. The Gentile audience must have wondered why they should welcome such a prospect, and have been even more puzzled when the missionaries went on to their next point. This was that the promised Messiah had appeared in the person of Jesus, who, so far from being victorious in battle, had been crucified as a rebel against Rome. To explain and justify this paradox the missionaries would have then had to explain that the original Messianic concept was faulty and too narrow. The Messiah was properly destined, not only to redeem Israel and free it from foreign oppression, but to be the spiritual saviour of all mankind. And, finally, they had to declare that their claim that Jesus was this higher figure was proved by the fact of his resurrection – the point we might have thought they would have begun with.

There was a considerable and three-fold development in thought here. Devout Jews, well read in the Old Testament, would indeed have looked forward to the rule of God on earth, but partly at least through a physical process of military conquest, much as Communists envisaged the triumph of Marxism coming through the expansion of the Soviet sphere. The chosen people would still be the elect, and 'some more equal than others'. Whereas Christianity was internationalist in doctrine, Judaism, even in its most enlightened form, was fundamentally nationalist.

Christianity was also more individualist. Like the original Messianism, it looked forward to a new world order; but this was to come about through a change of heart and mind in multitudinous individuals, through a moral and religious process. The growth of the Kingdom of God was to come gradually, compared in a familiar hymn to an accumulation of 'many drops of water, many grains of sand.'

Most fundamental of all was the new doctrine that Jesus' crucifixion had been a redeeming sacrifice, not merely for his own people but for the whole world. This was to add a fresh and revolutionary dimension to the traditional picture of the Messiah. It implied that Jesus was to be regarded as more than an ordinary human being.

We have to ask from where and how the disciples could have reached such a conclusion. As ordinary Jews they would not have thought of the Messiah as the son of God except in a metaphorical sense; and, having come to see Jesus as the promised Messiah, they would still have regarded him as a man, though one specially and uniquely favoured by God. His miracles of exorcism and healing would not have altered this view. They were merely the signs that were commonly demanded of a Messianic claimant to prove the genuineness of his pretensions. They would have been seen, not as miracles performed directly *by* Jesus, but as having been performed by God *through* him as God's chosen instrument. The disciples were slow to see Jesus as anything more, and in Mark 8. 17ff. we find Jesus taxing them with a failure to recognise his true status. For them to conceive of him as the universal saviour of the whole human race, a new factor had to be involved. It is logical to see this in his resurrection appearances.

We are not dealing now with the thought processes of Gentile converts. It has often been pointed out that the acceptance of Jesus as a divine saviour celebrated in the Christian eucharist was made easier for these by the existence in the Near East of a number of mystery religions. These commonly contained the figure of a dying god who rose to new life, and whose resurrection his worshippers hoped to share; and very commonly the means to this benefit for the elect was a form of communion rite whereby something of the virtue of the god passed to his worshippers. What concerns us is, not the reception that the Gentile world gave to the apostles' preaching, but how the latter themselves came to view Jesus in a new and larger light. Attempts have been made recently to portray Jesus as a purely Jewish figure, the last and greatest of the prophets and an ethical teacher of unique sublimity. But his disciples presented him to the world as much more than this. What, if not his resurrection, made them do so?

This attribution to Jesus of superhuman, and soon of divine status came with unique rapidity. It has been suggested[6] that a parallel is to be found in the way in which reverence for the Buddha Gautama passed ultimately into belief in his divinity. He also was no figure of myth or legend, but a genuinely historical person living towards the latter half of the sixth century B.C. – or about the same time as the Greek mathematician and philosopher Pythagoras. Always looked up to for his moral teaching and his holy life, his reputation continued to grow after his death, so that finally he came to be regarded as a god who had walked upon earth. However, his case and that of Jesus are not really similar. Gautama's elevation to godhead did not come until long after his life, about the same time as the rise of Christianity. His real person and character had by then retreated into the mists of time; and the legendary is always accorded the bonus of prestige. '*Omne ignotum pro magnifico*', said Tacitus. By contrast Jesus was recognised as the second person of the Trinity within a century of his crucifixion.

Nor are the divine honours accorded to Roman emperors very relevant. These might be thought to indicate that the Gentile world of Jesus' day was superstitiously ready to blur the distinction between god and man; so that, even if Christian missionaries did not cross the line, their non-Jewish audiences were temperamentally disposed to do so. But the ruler cult was more an expression of loyalty than of true worship. No one ever offered prayer or sacrifice to the divine Augustus or his successors in the hope of supernatural aid or favours. The emperors' subjects had their feet well on the ground; and none more firmly than the emperors themselves. Lying on his deathbed, the emperor Vespasian quipped ironically, '*Ut puto, deus fio.*' 'I guess I'm becoming a god'.

It is natural for those who have read of the mystery religions to wonder whether Christianity is simply just such another. At a lecture on them given by the leading Old Testament scholar S.A. Cook[7] this specific question was asked, and it is worth while to record his answer. All nations, he said, were granted so much divine revelation as they had capacity to receive. The capacity of the Greeks was great, and they accordingly had their Socrates and Plato and their mystery cults. Later the Arabs had their Mohammed. The most receptive people of all were the Jews, who were unique in being able to see the hand of God working in history; and they were, therefore, granted a uniquely full revelation. Only crude thinkers fancy that any body of theists has a monopoly of religious insight. It is not a matter of Christianity being no more valid than the mystery religions, but of both partaking of the truth.

Undoubtedly, however, the Near Eastern mystery cults and Greek philosophy had prepared the ground for Christian teaching. So also had the Persian religion of Zoroastrianism, which saw the universe as a battleground between the forces of light and darkness. And travel for missionaries had been made easier and safer by the existence of the Roman empire's Augustan peace. Pirates and brigands were forcefully suppressed, and the Roman roads served the needs of commerce and travellers as well as those of of the Roman legions. There were fewer obstacles to missionary work than in former centuries, and also than in some later ages.

Nevertheless the speed with which the Christian faith spread is impressive. Country dwellers (*pagani*) remained generally untouched and pagan; but within some twenty years of the Crucifixion in 30 A.D. Christian churches had been established in most of the main cities of the Near East, in Greece, and in Rome. We get the impression from the book of Acts that this achievement was mainly Paul's; but in passing we find mention of other propagandists. Paul was met in Corinth in 50 A.D. by

Aquila and Priscilla, who had been expelled from Rome along with other Jews. They seem to have been already Christians (converted perhaps by Peter). Thomas' mission to Parthia has already been mentioned (p. 116). Driven out from Jerusalem, the disciples took the new faith to Samaria, and the leader here was Philip. We hear also (Acts 18.24) of Apollos, who 'taught accurately the facts about Jesus, but knew only the baptism of John'.

This missionary work involved hardships and physical risk. Paul lists some in his second letter to the Corinthians (11.25ff): 'Five times the Jews gave me the thirty-nine strokes; three times I have been beaten with rods; once I was stoned; three times I have been shipwrecked, and for twenty-four hours I was adrift on the open sea.' In 64 A.D. the Neronian persecution began; and tradition relates that Peter and Paul were both executed for their faith on the same day; Peter by crucifixion, Paul, as a Roman citizen, by the sword. The disciples can only have outfaced such ordeals if they were themselves thoroughly persuaded of the truth of the Gospel they were proclaiming. It was paradoxical. To the Jews a crucified Messiah was a contradiction in terms, as impossible as a square circle. And they were all Jews. What, if not the Resurrection, caused them to make this leap of faith?

Curiously enough it is the indirect proofs of Jesus' resurrection that are the strongest part of the case. In default of it history has to explain why Jesus' fame did not die a natural death with his execution; how his followers' conception of him broadened and deepened from that of a merely Jewish Messiah to that of a universal saviour; and what psychological stimulus impelled them to embark on a campaign of international preaching mission. Such a project would be like trying to explain the extent of Islam if Mohammed's life had ended in ignominy and disgrace. Jesus' moral and ethical teaching, which modern Jewish scholarship finds something less than revolutionary,[8] does not seem a sufficient cause. We have to bite on the bullet of the supernatural.

The issue is similar to one addressed by Sherlock Holmes. Not having re-read the whole omnibus edition, I quote freely. 'When you have examined all the other possible solutions, and none seems adequate or satisfactory, then the last remaining one, however improbable or unlikely in itself, must be the correct one.'

The difficulty is that, in despite of logic, we are constitutionally programmed to jib at the improbable; so that natural doubts remain. These can only be dealt with pragmatically in a way suggested in the last chapter.

What Manner Of Man?

Supposing Jesus was raised, or rose, from the dead, what does this imply or prove about his nature? How did his first followers interpret the event? And what is its significance for us today?

One possible conclusion in the ancient world would have been that he was just such another semi-divine person as the legendary Hercules, who won full divinity by his services to mankind. The Great Twin Brethren, Castor and Pollux, were another instance of the type. They led the Romans to victory at the battle of Lake Regillus, and then, on their translation to the skies, became the divine guardians of sailors. The court poet Horace suggested that, as a benefactor of the human race, the Emperor Augustus was destined also to join the company of the gods on Mount Olympus, where he would quaff the hallowed nectar with ruby lips.[1] Some of his Near Eastern subjects might indeed think in that way.

But not the Jews. And it is with Jesus' Jewish contemporaries that we are first concerned. There were no semi-divine persons in Jewish thinking. On the contrary, the distinction between man and God was sharp and firmly insisted on. In John's account of Jesus' trial before Pilate the Jews are reported as saying, 'We have a law; and by that law he ought to die, because he has claimed to be the Son of God.' Whatever doubts any scholar may have about the course of the trial, this must surely reflect the Jewish thought of the period. Jesus' disciples would not, therefore, have been so easily disposed to deify their dead master as were the

130

Syrians and Paphlagonians to pay such honour to the deceased Augustus.

Brandon goes further,[2] and suggests that even a belief in Jesus' resurrection would not necessarily have inspired in them the further belief in his divinity. He argues that they differed from other Jews mainly in believing that Jesus was a prophet who had died a martyr's death, had been raised from the dead, and would return to restore the kingdom to Israel – in much the same way as King Arthur was expected by some to reappear and repel the Saxon invader: *rex quondam et futurus*: 'the past and future king'. Jews fancied that Elijah would reappear on earth to behold the coming Messiah (Matt. 17.10); but no one supposed that Elijah was divine. We tend to think that resurrection implies divinity; but to the Jews it may not have done.

Certainly the disciples reached their conclusions about the risen Christ only gradually. In Peter's first address to the crowds at Pentecost (Acts 2) he claimed only that Jesus was indeed the Messiah and that this was proved by his having been raised from the dead. Then in his second speech, he added prophecies of a suffering, not military, Messiah. A more developed theology comes later, in Paul's letters. Even in them there are few unambiguous attributions of divinity to Christ.[3] Yet there are numerous mentions of him as the human race's Saviour.[4] And this surely involves supra-human status. Yet Peter had begun by saying that Jesus was '*a man*' pointed out by God through the miracles he was given power to perform; and this view was never abandoned, was never displaced by the other. Jesus was held to have had two natures, both human and divine, and to have been at once both God and man. And, as it became more organised, the Church resolutely insisted that this was so.

In the early days of the Faith, however, there were some Christians who thought that Jesus was really God in disguise, cloaked in human form and moving about among men, but all the time a supernatural being. He merely *seemed* to be man: essentially he had no part in human nature. The idea peeps out in a Christmas hymn:

Veiled in flesh the Godhead see.
Hail the incarnate Deity.

This became known as the Doketist heresy, so named from the Greek verb *dokein*, 'to seem'. It coloured *The Gospel of Peter*, which speaks of Jesus as 'feeling no pain' upon the cross, whereas orthodox theology regarded the suffering involved in Jesus' crucifixion as the means of its saving power. The book was accordingly denounced as erroneous,[5] and was not given the imprimatur of acceptance into the canon. If Jesus were indeed God posing and masquerading as a man, his resurrection would have been no wonder or miracle at all. It might have served to demonstrate God's existence (something which no one then doubted). But it could confer no benefit on mankind. And this the Christians were convinced that it did.

Going to the opposite end of the spectrum, some have regarded Jesus as a person inspired by the spirit of God to a unique degree, but still no more than human. Unlike the rest of us he was entirely selfless and continuously in contact with the divine. And his resurrection was both a tribute to this character in him and a kind of spiritual breakthrough, analogous to Roger Bannister's running the four-minute mile. This success enabled others to repeat and equal the feat; and similarly Christ's own triumph over sin and death was a forerunner for that of others. Again, his influence might be compared to the slipstream of a racing car that pulls others along behind it. But, if that is the whole story, it is a sad lookout for most of the human race, who, morally speaking, would be hard put to it to run even a seven-minute mile, and whose spiritual cars are not racing models. All that could be claimed is that Christ has shown the way for others to follow; and their success or failure would still depend upon themselves and their own merits. The only Gospel text that can be quoted in support of this interpretation is the sentence attributed to Jesus in John 12.32: 'I shall draw all men to myself, when I am lifted up from the earth.' What is not clear is the mechanism of such assistance.

The orthodox explanation of this aid is given in the doctrine of the Atonement and in the teaching that Jesus was at once both Perfect God and Perfect Man. In the words of the children's hymn:[6]

> There was no other good enough
>> To pay the price of sin.
> He only could unlock the gate
>> Of Heaven and let us in.

It should be noted that there is a close connection between the doctrine of the Atonement and that of the Virgin Birth. For Christ to be God Incarnate there had to be some kind of miracle. And if he were not God Incarnate the Crucifixion would have had no redeeming power.

The doctrine of the Atonement is too often presented in a way calculated to deter rather than attract the prospective convert. Hot gospellers speak of Jesus willingly suffering the penalty for our sins, of his taking our guilt upon himself and they quote Isaiah 53: 'By his stripes we are healed'. The Crucifixion is pictured as an instance of vicarious suffering and of Jesus' being made the scapegoat for others' wrongdoing. In the crude modern phrase he is portrayed as the fall guy, and God as an angry Jehovah who had to be appeased.

Just how inadequate is this popular version of the Atonement becomes obvious if we consider what some may feel is a blasphemous comparison. Suppose that that famous headmaster, Dr Arnold, had discovered some serious misdemeanour to which none of the boys would own up, and had threatened a collective punishment; and then that his own son, rather than that the whole school should be punished, had offered to accept a flogging himself; and that Dr Arnold, while praising this self-sacrifice, had accepted the proposed solution. What would we think of such a headmaster? We should be calling for his resignation.

It is a scandalous picture. And yet there are not a few texts in Paul's letters and in that addressed to the Hebrews from which a similar interpretation might be gathered. 'The wrath of God is revealed from heaven against all ungodliness' (Rom. 1.18); but '(Jesus) delivered us from the wrath to come' (1 Thess. 1.10). He 'gave himself for our sins' (Gal. 1.4), and 'put away sin by the sacrifice of himself' (Heb. 9.14). 'He was given up to death for our misdeeds' (Rom. 4.25); and '(God) did not spare his own son, but gave him up for us all' (Rom. 8.32). In these passages Jesus seems to be thought of a kind of whipping boy, and God, not as a kindly Miss Do-As-You-Would-Be-Done-By, but as a grim Mrs Be-Done-By-As-You-Did.

It appears that, as Jews, the disciples interpreted Jesus' Passion in the light of an Old Testament and traditional Judaic frame of reference. In Hebrew sin and debt were expressed by the same word, and any wrongdoing or transgression of the Mosaic code incurred a debt to God, which had to be paid through sacrifice or by charitable almsgiving. Once a year the High Priest, descended from Aaron, sacrificed a goat as a sin offering for the whole people. Its blood was a means of purification and a washing away of sin. Jesus' sacrifice of himself was thought to be parallel; and the parallel is fully worked out in Chapter 9 of the Letter to the Hebrews. This is paraphrased in a nineteenth century hymn:

> For, as the priest of Aaron's line
>   Within the Holiest stood,
> And sprinkled all the mercy-shrine
>   With sacrificial blood;

So He, who once atonement wrought,
  Our priest of endless power,
Presents himself for those He bought
  In that dark noontide hour.

There is a significant change of emphasis here from Paul's letters. The writer speaks, not of 'penalty', but of 'sacrifice'. The Letter to the Hebrews was penned rather later than Paul's, and already the doctrine is being refined. There can be sacrifices apart from any context of guilt or retribution. The young men who gave their lives in the world wars were *sacrificing* them for civilisation's gain, but not, in most minds, as a vicarious penalty for politicians' crimes. In the last century other members of a Scottish family would make *sacrifices* so that the ablest could go to university. Captain Oates *sacrificed* his own life so that the other members of Scott's ill-fated polar expedition could survive; he was not attempting to redeem them from their sins. The essence of sacrifice is the surrender of something of value, generally for the sake of a greater good.

This is one important modification of the whipping boy picture of Isaiah 53. Another is the notion that Jesus was in some way a representative or sample of the whole race. 'A consecrating priest and those whom he consecrates are all of one stock' (Hebrews 2.11), and therefore Jesus 'had to be made like these brothers of his in every way to expiate the sins of the people' (Hebrews 2. 17). The idea is that whatever Jesus suffered or achieved would also be suffered or. achieved by everyone else. His sacrifice would effectively be theirs as well, and his conquest of death theirs also. In Paul's words, 'As in Adam all die, even so in Christ shall all be made alive' (1 Cor. 15.20). At first sight this is argument by analogy; and argument by analogy is notoriously fallacious. But that is not the disciples' line of thought. They believed that through baptism Christians were spiritually united and identified with Christ, so that they were already in this life inheritors of the Kingdom of Heaven. The thought is not analogical but mystical.

The disciples' exposition of the doctrine of Atonement is not entirely consistent. Sometimes they speak of Jesus' taking upon himself the burden of the multitude of human *sins*; in other passages they claim that by his self-sacrifice he freed the human race from its *sinfulness*. Both formulations are open to criticism. The first is easily intelligible, but morally abhorrent. The latter inspires awe, but is barely comprehensible. And in practice it shades into the first. The Church of England catechism describes baptism as a death unto sin; but it does not maintain that those admitted into the Church by baptism will never sin again. Presumably, then, it is held that Jesus atoned on the Cross both for past and future sins.

So vicarious suffering is still part of the picture. In the words of the First letter of John (2.2), Christ is 'the propitiation for our sins.' We are still dealing with an angry Jehovah who demands his pound of flesh in retribution for sin committed. The doctrine smacks of what was later branded as the heresy of tritheism. This assumes the existence, not of one God, but of three – three separate beings: Father, Son and Holy Spirit. In the Palm Sunday hymn the conception becomes explicit:

> The Father on his sapphire throne
> Awaits his own anointed Son.

Only too clearly the faithful are encouraged to think of a God 'up there' and a Son 'down here.' It is in fact very difficult to conceive of the doctrine of the Atonement except in tritheist terms. But, as soon as one begins to, the moral qualms keep coming back. Perhaps it was as a result of this that the doctrine of the Trinity was evolved, which the Athanasian creed terms incomprehensible, though not in the popular sense of that word. A better translation of the Latin might be 'beyond human conception.' The doctrine was not officially proclaimed until

325 A.D. at the Council of Nicaea, but could have been held in embryo long before. 'I don't understand the doctrine of the Trinity' an Irish confirmation candidate once said to his priest. 'You're not meant to understand it,' was the reply; 'it's a mystery.' A very good theological answer, to be sure; but not of much help to the inquiring layman. Bishop Robinson was surely right to call for a reformulation of the doctrine of the Atonement in fresh, untraditional terms. We need not now feel bound to interpret Jesus' passion and resurrection in the thought patterns of first-century Judaism.

Jesus himself almost directly rejected them. He taught that God would freely pardon the repentant sinner without any requirement of prior or accompanying penalty or penance. The prodigal's father demanded no earnest of future good behaviour, but straight away killed the fatted calf in his honour. The tax-gatherer is justified in his prayer merely because of his humility. The woman taken in adultery was told only to go and sin no more. And the prostitute who anointed Jesus and dried his feet with her hair (Luke 7.36-48) was told simply that her sins were forgiven. In none of these instances, whether in parable or in life, do we find any demand of a penance or a suggestion that punishment of sin is a precondition for salvation. As we have seen (p. 103 above), it was precisely Jesus' willingness to welcome the sinner without demanding any prior evidence of reform that set him at variance with the Pharisees.

With all these parables or incidents in mind, we should be surprised to find Jesus describing his coming death as a sacrifice to secure forgiveness of sin for his followers. Yet his words at the Last Supper, as reported in the Church of England eucharist service, do precisely that. The quotation there, however, is not completely accurate. Our earliest account comes in Paul's First Letter to the Corinthians (11.23ff):

'The Lord Jesus, on the night of his arrest, took bread and, after giving thanks to God, broke it and said: "This is my body, which is for you; do this as a memorial of me." In the same way, he took the cup after supper, and said: "This cup is the new covenant sealed by my blood. Whenever you drink it, do this as a memorial of me."'

Mark 14.24 has 'This is my blood, the blood of the covenant, shed for many.' Luke 22.17 has only 'Take this and share it among yourselves.' Only Matthew has 'This is my blood, the blood of the covenant, shed for many *for the forgiveness of sins*.' (Matt. 26.28). (My italics). If the last phrase is authentic, we should have expected Paul to have reported it along with the rest. It is not consonant with Jesus' previous teaching, and so may be taken to be a gloss and addition by the early Church.

Our modern aversion to the concept of Jesus submitting himself to be a scapegoat (in the popular sense of the word: the original scapegoat was symbolically chased off out of the community, bearing the guilt of all the people upon him[8]) – this is not the only objection to the traditional doctrine. There is also a philosophic one, in that Jesus/God could have had no certainty that he would indeed be condemned and executed. The High Priest and all the other members of the Sanhedrin were free agents, at liberty to cast their votes either way. And Pilate was not bound to endorse their verdict. According to the Gospel accounts he showed a reluctance to do so, suggesting at one point that he let Jesus off with a flogging. Suppose he had dismissed the case, or that, by some miraculous change of heart, the High Priest had decided not to prosecute, how would events have turned out then? Entering Jerusalem as he did, Jesus was putting his head in the lion's mouth. But supposing the lion did not bite?

This is another difficulty in the orthodox doctrine of the Atonement. Yet one of its articles is a true and valid perception. This is the belief in Man's inherent sinfulness and moral imperfection. Unfortunately, with the passage from Isaiah in their minds, Jesus' disciples combined the conception of a triumph over Sin with that of a redeeming sacrifice for the remission of a multitude of sins. And then, relying upon what it thought was the inspired teaching of the apostles, the mediaeval Church continued to teach that Jesus' crucifixion was a kind of ransom paid to the Devil for the human race, whose lives were forfeit because of their misdeeds. (The idea appears again in C.S. Lewis' children's book *The Lion, the Witch and the Wardrobe*.) This was an unhappy encrustation upon what was originally a sound and well-formed conception.

It is not only Christians and Jews who have spoken of an essential defect in human nature. We no longer believe in the Noble Savage, untainted by the corrupt ways of the city. Nor, since the murder of James Bulger by two other boys not yet in their teens, can we believe in the innocence of youth. The author of the novel *The Lord of the Flies* saw differently. The book tells how, when marooned upon a desert island, a group of cathedral choristers degenerate into tyranny and sadism. As a schoolmaster he knew his boys; and actual events have confirmed his vision. It is a rare school in which there is absolutely no bullying; and unpleasant tendencies exist from an early age.

In the early years of this century progressive thinkers ascribed crime to social causes. Then war and the invention of atomic bombs brought a change of emphasis. It became fashionable among writers to suggest that Man's moral development was lagging behind his technical mastery. The theme is developed at length in Arthur Koestler's *The Ghost in the Machine*. He summarises as follows:

> When one contemplates the streak of insanity running through human history, it appears highly probable that *homo sapiens* is a biological freak, the result of some mistake in the evolutionary process. The ancient doctrine of original sin, variants of which occur independently in the mythologies of diverse cultures, could be a reflection of man's awareness of his own inadequacy, of the intuitive hunch that somewhere along the line of his ascent something has gone wrong.[9]

He maintains that there is inadequate coordination between the older and the more recently formed sections of our brains, between the ancient and primitive portion and the later developed human and rational part.

The book may be considered to be a biological update of Plato's theory of the tripartite soul. Plato theorised that the human soul consisted of three elements: (1) the human and rational, (2) the spirited (which he allegorised as a lion), and (3) the lustful and appetitive (likened to a many-headed monster, each head representing a different craving or desire). In a well-integrated personality (to use a modern term) the second, lion-like element, with its generous, honourable instincts, would be the ally of the first, human, element; but there was always the danger that the second, or even the third, section might dominate. Similarly Koestler believes that the neo-mammalian section of our human brains may gain control, and that our generous, altruistic impulses and instincts may paradoxically be the cause of social and historical disaster.

Koestler sees the universe as constructed on a modular, holistic pattern, with each holon (his own coinage) both a unit existing in its own right and as a part in a larger whole. As such it has both self-assertive and self-transcending tendencies. The biological pattern is repeated at the sociological level, with each clan, tribe or nation looking both inwards and outwards. And the tragedy of history is that our self-transcending, altruistic emotions and urges have been repeatedly harnessed by deluded, yet self-interested leaders for destructive ends. We are encouraged (to use Goebbels' phrase) to 'think with our blood' and to accept closed systems of thought which it is taboo to question.

This is a very plausible analysis of the ideological movements of recent times, although, even here, not the whole story; and it could be subjected to detailed criticisms with regard to previous centuries. But what is relevant to the present chapter is Koestler's insight of 'a paranoid streak running though human history' and of a fundamental flaw in humankind which developed with their emergence from their primate ancestors. In opposition to Christianity, he attributes the world's major troubles not to selfish, but to self-sacrificing impulses. But in fact the way in which people's nobler emotions can be perverted to serve baser ends is part of the evidence of a fundamental defect in the human psyche. Readers of Milton will recall that 'out of good still to find means of evil' was part of Satan's strategy.

As evidence of original, birth sin in mankind, one might produce a long catalogue of crime. But it would not be much to the purpose; for the point at issue is, not the depravity of felons, but the moral failings of the whole human race. So better, more decisive evidence of these is the sad tendency of well-meaning idealists to resort, in order to achieve their aims, to the most scandalous means. This ruthlessness is not always attributable to emotional stress.

The behaviour of animals' rights protesters offers a very relevant example. Most of those who demonstrated against the maltreatment of veal calves in 1995 were peaceful citizens. But some broke lorry windows and assaulted the drivers. Then butchers' windows were smashed, and arson attacks made on milk tankers and depots. A group calling itself the Justice Department sent incendiary devices and mousetraps loaded with razor blades through the post. No one can plausibly maintain that the perpetrators of these actions had been driven to extremes. What the events illustrate is that even persons inspired by the noblest of motives have their feet of clay.

The same retrogression has occurred in the wider political field. The I.R.A. was originally inspired with the stirring vision of a united Ireland. Then from escalation to escalation it came to knee-capping and indiscriminate bombing. Earlier in history the French Revolution began with the cry of Liberty, Equality and Fraternity – and ended with the entertainment of the guillotine and the Reign of Terror. The Communist Manifesto, penned by

Marx and Engels, is full of moral fervour; and the Party attracted young men from wealthy families with nothing personal to gain from the overthrow of capitalism. Yet when it came to putting theory into practice in Russia, socialism swerved off course, with Stalin slaying as many as, and more than, Hitler. There was similar disillusion in England over the Cromwellian revolution. By the time the monarchy was restored in 1660, people were heartily sick of the rule of the colonels.

There are thus a number of instances in history of noble endeavours turning sour; and this fact suggests that there is something fundamentally at fault in Man's moral make-up. One body of visionaries after another is seen to have abandoned its original principles. The recurrent motif implies that there is an inherent defect in the human race.

Another, more homely indication of moral imperfection may be found in the existence of the word *ought*. People use it to indicate that some standard of conduct or duty has not been fulfilled. Children watching television may be uneasily aware that they *ought* to be doing homework; their mothers may feel that they *ought* to have done more house-cleaning; and their fathers may think guiltily that they *ought* to have stayed in the office that afternoon instead of going off to watch football. In all these instances the persons involved know well enough what their obligations are, but find the execution of them uncongenial. There is what Paul referred to as the war in the members. In other words we are all hobbled with original sin.

It might, of course, be argued that these feelings of moral obligation have been instilled into us by Society. And that is largely true. However, the point does not really affect the argument. The conclusion remains that Man has a natural, inborn disinclination to follow the path of duty.

Following Paul, orthodox theologians have held that this tendency in Man to sin stems from his freedom of will. O.C.

Quick's analysis is typical.[10] Alone of the animal world, he declares, Man possesses the power of rational and deliberate choice. 'Within limits Man can choose both the ends of his action and the means whereby he pursues them, and in doing so exercises a purposive control over his environment, over nature, over his fellow creatures, and even over himself.' The actions of other animals are dictated purely by instinct; but Man has a free and spiritual will. Yet this very freedom meant that the first man could act in a manner contrary to God's will, and when he did so he impaired his own moral nature and that of all his descendants.

'As in Adam all died', wrote Paul. It is interesting to note that this theory of inherited moral weakness is echoed by some modern biologists, who believe that criminal tendencies may be due to inherited genes. Some persons may indeed be born for the gallows.

Some of this thinking may require revision and modification. In the 1950s psychologists believed that the behaviour of animals was entirely ruled by inborn instincts, and they would dismiss the organised and complicated life-structures of bees and ants as no evidence to the contrary. Recently, however, there was shown on television the success of a squirrel in surmounting a long obstacle course so as to reach some desired food. This surely argued a deliberate intelligence. And Koestler gives examples of intelligent improvisation by digger wasps when their traditional methods of feeding their young are frustrated and of honey bees switching roles so as to maintain the life of the hive. One may also wonder what orthodox and traditionalist theologians would have made of beavers' dam-building. What is this but an adaptation of the environment for their own ends? All these examples suggest that rational intelligence is not a gift peculiar to Man, but is developed in varying degrees in other animals. If so, Man is not the only being capable of frustrating God's design, and this may be what Paul meant by declaring that 'the whole creation groaneth and travaileth' (Rom. 8.22). Original sin may have infected more than Man.

But this is a digression. The essence of sin is reckless self-assertion regardless of the rights of other beings, with whom God willed us to live in harmony. It is displayed in self-regardant aggression and lust for domination, and in this mood rides roughshod over the rights of others. It is the opposite of love.

One uses this word with hesitation, since the word has become debased so as to mean often little more than sexual attraction. The Greek for that is *eros*. The quality the Gospels speak of is *agape*. This is not emotional or passionate love, but a disinterested, deliberate desire for another's good. It is not a mere maudlin affection and sentimentality, or a genial sentiment of goodwill, and can as well be bestowed upon an unsightly beggar as upon a beautiful girl. It may develop into an emotion, but it begins as a moral attitude. There is love – and love: one word for two distinct and not necessarily connected things. Sexual love can be selfish love; the essence of *agape* is unselfishness. It is this distinction that Blake writes of in *The Clod and the Pebble*.

> 'Love seeketh not Itself to please,
> Nor for itself hath any care,
> But for another gives its ease,
> And builds a Heaven in Hell's despair.'
>
> So sung a little Clod of Clay
> Trodden with the cattle's feet,
> But a Pebble of the brook
> Warbled out these metres meet:
>
> 'Love seeketh only Self to please,
> To bind another to Its delight,
> Joys in another's loss of ease,
> And builds a Hell in Heaven's despite.'

It is through selflessness, through *agape*, that we become at one with God, that we gain atonement. But ordinary people will never achieve complete mastery over their self-regardant impulses. To gain salvation we shall need some bonus points, some more than others, so as to make the grade. But Jesus was perfectly selfless, perfectly at one with God, and so his image on earth. In John's words (14.9) 'Anyone who has seen me (Jesus) has seen the Father.' So much was he in accord with God that, as he lived his life, it could be said that God was moving about among men. That is the manner of man he was; and in virtue of this unique sympathy with the Divine, he was more than an ordinary human.

The objection may be made that an assumption has been made in this last paragraph, and that we know very little of Jesus' life and character as opposed to his teaching. There is a measure of truth in this. Contrary to Mrs Alexander's Christmas hymn, his 'wondrous childhood' is almost a complete blank to us; and her assertion that he would always honour and obey his mother may chiefly tell us what qualities Victorian parents looked for in their offspring. Luke's story of his conversing with the doctors in the Temple indicates an early religious awareness; but up to the time of his baptism that is all. The fact that he lived the life of an itinerant preacher from then on with 'nowhere to lay his head' proves that he gave wealth and comfort a low priority compared with other things; and his Cleansing of the Temple demonstrates a moral courage to challenge accepted tradition. This is all we know directly. The main evidence of his personality comes from the impression he made on others.

His disciples were so affected by the force and tone of his teaching as to leave their various trades and join in his mission; Mary Magdalene was induced to reverse her whole manner of life; and even Pilate, who might have been expected to give short shrift to a humble provincial, hesitated a great deal before acquiescing in the chief priests' demand for his execution. His willingness to face death and execution is proof of absolute

145

disregard of self. To believe that his teaching was reflected in his life seems a fair inference.

This leads on to the primary significance of his resurrection. It was a triumphant endorsement and vindication of his teaching and conduct. His self-sacrifice on the cross was a supreme example of self-denial and of a determination to act as he believed God wished; and his resurrection is the proof that such dedication and altruism will find its reward. He blazed the trail and showed the spirit in which people must live if they hope for salvation. And insofar as they adhere to the pattern he set, they can, always with the help of God's grace, merit survival beyond the grave. As he said, his own life was the Way.

Resurrection does not in itself prove his divinity. Nor do the miracles recorded in the Gospels. There have been other instances of faith-healing since then, though of increasing rarity; and no one would consider the agents to whom they are credited more than human. His acts of healing may be considered to have been performed, not *by* him, but by God *through* him, or by powers granted to him by God. In themselves they prove nothing about his nature or status.

The same can be said of his ethical teaching. 'In his ethical code,' wrote the Jewish author Joseph Klausner, 'there is a sublimity, distinctiveness and originality in form unparalleled in any other Hebrew ethical code; neither is there any parallel to the art of his parables.' Professor Vermes[11] quotes this tribute with approval and goes on to speak of Jesus' profundity of insight and grandeur of character. But neither he nor Klausner believes Jesus to have been more than man.

I have attempted, up to Jesus' last week, to present a narrative consistent with this view, so that the reader may suspend judgment. It is in line with the facts as recorded. So far as their evidence is concerned, we should be justified in regarding Jesus as a man uniquely inspired and guided by God, a person in intimate contact with his Creator, and absolutely ready to do his will, but yet no more than a man. But there is one overwhelming difficulty. This interpretation would imply that God had prompted and directed an innocent man to court death by the barbarous method of crucifixion. And that I regard as a blasphemy.

In this way we are brought back to the orthodox doctrine that Jesus was both human and divine. He himself claimed as much in his last words before the Sanhedrin (Mark 14.62): 'You will see the Son of Man seated at the right hand of Power and coming with the clouds of heaven.' And this was an occasion when a prudent self-concern might have tempted him to under-statement, to represent himself as no more than the last in a line of prophets. The only way to dismiss this piece of evidence is to impugn the Gospel text and its historical accuracy at this point. Against this passage can be set Jesus' last words upon the cross, 'My God, my God, why hast thou forsaken me?' They seem to imply a clear distinction between himself and God, so that the two texts stand in stark opposition to each other. Either we have to consider that Jesus' claim to divinity was a deluded and unfounded claim or to explain his last cry as a moment of temporary weakness wrung from his human side by extreme agony. He *had* this human side. In the Garden of Gethsemane before his arrest the threat and prospect of suffering made him sweat blood; and this suggests that he was peculiarly sensitive to pain. If so, he would have been the more under pressure to abase himself before the Council. But he did not. On balance (and it must be admitted that the balance is very fine) the traditional view has the advantage.

If we accept this, that Jesus was both Perfect God and Perfect Man, then we have also to accept the doctrine of the Trinity. Otherwise we believe there to be more than one God and fall into the heresy of tritheism. To avoid this, we should recognise that the traditional terms of God the Father and God the Son are only metaphors, good enough for children and for the

147

childhood of the human race, but not for adults. In earlier, less sophisticated centuries they may have been helpful; but they have now become obsolete and misleading. More appropriate terms for today might be God-in-the-Timeless and God-in-Time.

About 1 B.C. God decided to intervene decisively in history by giving a further revelation of himself and by entering our world of Time in his own person. For this purpose he performed deliberate self-limitation. He was not to be omnipresent. So Jesus was a man living in a particular town in the country of Palestine. Nor was Jesus omniscient. He was not able to foretell the date of his second coming with complete accuracy. He lived only in a certain year and age, knowing of the past only through recorded history and of the future only through wise and imaginative calculation. He could be weary and need to sleep. And he could, finally, suffer pain and death. But death and resurrection abolished these limitations, as John (16.7) saw. 'If I do not go, your Advocate will not come; whereas if I go, I will send him to you.' Only through Jesus' death could his spirit transcend its earthly limitations. Through the Crucifixion God-in-Time won free from the bonds he had voluntarily imposed on himself.

The disciples and, following them, the Church since have believed that the Crucifixion was also a victory over Sin as a cosmic force. No one before then had been able to resist its power and temptation. But Jesus was able to, consistently and completely, and finally in this last trial and ordeal. And this achievement was somehow a breakthrough which permanently altered the spiritual landscape. Sin still remains; but its cutting edge has been irreparably blunted. To vary the metaphor, it has been permanently crippled in the encounter. We are in the realms of the mystical here, where ordinary logic cannot cope. It is a formulation that we can only accept through a leap of faith. It cannot be proved or disproved.

It was not just God's son upon the Cross. It was truly God himself; and the event demonstrated in symbolic fashion that he can empathise with his suffering creatures. He is not aloof from the world, like Zeus upon a remote Olympus, but regards the fall of a sparrow; and all our hairs are numbered (Matt. 10.30). So, since sin must always involve injury to another, it must also cause pain to God. He will be distressed, as a mother is distressed by the sight of an injury to her child. This is stated explicitly in the parable of the Sheep and the Goats (Matt. 25.31–46). Disregard of our fellows is also disregard of God. In this way Jesus did, and does, suffer for the sins of the whole world. But not as a scapegoat. That crude and primitive picture is one we should abandon.

God-in-the Timeless became God-in-Time, we have said; or, in the words of John's first chapter, 'the Word was made flesh.' According to Matthew and Luke, this came about through the miracle of the Virgin Birth. So, logically, we have next to examine their birth narratives.

THE BIRTH NARRATIVES

Up and down the country before Christmas primary schools produce a play combining extracts from Matthew and Luke into a composite narrative. It begins with the angel Gabriel's announcement to Mary that she is to bear a son who will be king over Israel, moves on to the decree of the Emperor Augustus that all the (Roman) world should be registered, to Joseph and Mary's consequent journey to Bethlehem, and so to the tale of the three wise men and to King Herod's alarm. The incidents fit together plausibly enough – until we consult students of ancient history. We then discover that according to the traditional dating Herod died in 4 B.C. and the census conducted by Quirinius as governor of Syria was not held until 6 A.D., or some 10 years later.

And this is not the only difficulty in the Gospel narratives. No mention has been found in any other writer of the general census that Luke's narrative seems to tell of; it is questionable whether any Roman taxes (to which the census might be preliminary) were levied in vassal states like Herod's; and scholars assert that there would have been no need for Joseph to travel the 70 odd miles to his ancestral home to register. A villager in Nazareth would more regularly have been required to proceed for the purpose to the chief town in his residential district – Sepphoris.[1] Attempts have been made to save Luke's credit by pointing to regulations in the neighbouring province of Egypt that for census and registration purposes persons should return to their *idia*; but this need not mean to the homes of their ancestors. Its natural meaning is that those away from home on business should return and register in their normal areas. As it stands, Luke's account makes little sense.

These commonsense considerations are reinforced when we consider the structure of Roman taxation. The main provincial tax was the *tributum soli*, a land tax. Registration at the home of one's forebears would not at all have helped in its assessment. Nor would it for the purposes of the other tax, the *tributum capitis*. Contrary to its wording, this was not a poll tax, but a levy on forms of property other than land, such as cattle and slaves. Altogether an instruction for Palestine's inhabitants to post back and forth for a census would seem bizarre,

These considerations affecting the detailed accuracy of the Gospel birth narratives have prompted sceptics to claim that they are total fictions; Matthew's designed to explain why the family had moved from Bethlehem to Nazareth, and Luke's how a child of Galilean parents came to be born in Bethlehem. The suggestion has also been made that they were concocted with details culled from the Old Testament prophecies:

> Behold, a virgin shall conceive . . . (Isaiah 7.14)
> But thou, Bethlehem Ephratah, though thou be little among the thousands of Judah, yet out of thee shall he come forth unto me that is to be ruler in Israel. (Micah 5.2)
> Kings shall come to the brightness of thy rising. (Isaiah 60.3)
> Rachel weeping for her children . . . (Jeremiah 31.15)
> Out of Egypt have I called my son. (Hosea 11.1)

Some of this, though, is careless scholarship. In Isaiah 7.14 the correct translation of the original Hebrew (*almah*) is not 'virgin', but 'young woman.' The three wise men were not kings until mediaeval times, but astrologers, perhaps even Jewish astrologers, descended from Israelites who had remained in Babylon after the enforced Captivity. Sharper eyes have also noticed that Matthew has altered Micah's 'ruler' to 'shepherd.' Was this, perhaps, because he knew that Jesus was indeed born in Bethlehem but had to massage the words of the prophecy to fit with history? He has a tendency to quote rather freely from memory for evangelistic purposes.

The contention that vassal states were not subject to Roman taxation is not unchallenged. We know from the Roman historian Tacitus[2] that in 36 A.D. in the client kingdom of Cappadocia the rebellious tribe of the Cietae was refusing to pay tribute, and that Roman forces were called in to assist the king's troops. The case of Herod's kingdom is less clear. According to Josephus[3] Pompey imposed tribute upon the territory during his overall command in the Near East. But then, we read, Caesar exempted Antipater, Herod's father, from taxation.[4] There soon came another change. After the defeat of Caesar's assassins at the battle of Philippi, control of the eastern section of the Empire fell to Mark Antony, and the Greek historian Appian records that he imposed a tribute on Herod when appointing him king.[5] As astute a timeserver as the Vicar of Bray, Herod managed to salvage his position when his overlord Antony and Cleopatra's forces were defeated by those of Octavian/Augustus; but it would be surprising if Augustus hurried to emulate Julius Caesar's generosity towards a prince who had backed his rival. What is certainly clear is that the imposition of Roman taxation upon a client kingdom was not unusual; and a passage in Josephus indicates that the Jews may have had to pay Roman taxes in Herod's lifetime. He tells us that in the early days of his successor's reign the crowd clamoured for the abolition of the purchase tax. This looks like the Roman *centesima rerum venalium* or 1% levy on sales. But it does not follow that the whole range of Roman taxes was imposed at once. 'A wise conqueror', wrote Hitler, 'will impose his demands in stages.' Augustus was no less shrewd.

The problem of dates is less easily dealt with. At first Christian writers tried to maintain that Quirinius had had two terms as governor of Syria, translating Luke 2.1 as 'This was the first registration in the time when Quirinius was governor.' But the only possible proof of this comes from what is known as The Headless Inscription. This records that some unknown gentleman (the name is missing) was twice (*iterum*) governor of Syria. But there can be no certainty when this appointment was made. It could have been in another century!

A more probable solution was offered by J. Thorley in the journal *Greece and Rome*.[6] Adopting an American scholar's contention that Herod did not die until 1 B.C., he goes on to note that the year 3/2 B.C. was something like a jubilee year for the emperor Augustus, to be marked by celebrations. Augustus had conferred on him the title of Pater Patriae, 'Father of the Nation'; and it looks as if oaths of allegiance were organised throughout the Empire. (Some Pharisees refused compliance.[7]) Along with these might have gone a population count. Together with a written memorial of his own acts the Emperor also bequeathed at his death a *breviarium imperii* containing a short statement of all the resources of the Roman State, and including the number of the population of citizens, subjects and allies. It was in fact a handbook to the statistics of the Roman empire. It is easy to believe that such an account was compiled for propagandist and ceremonial purposes in Augustus' jubilee year; (for Augustus was a master of propaganda.) What is odd, however, is that no ancient historian records the exercise – only the result. Except Luke (1.2), who seems to confuse an Empire-wide registration with the purely local 6 A.D. census in Judaea. The latter was commonly termed 'the census' just as 'the war' now means the second world war; and for precision Luke should have written, 'This was the first registration, before that when Quirinius was governor.' But that is not our present text.

This registration could have been left to provincial governors' deputies to organise, while their superiors attended the jubilee ceremonies in Rome; and it is possible that Quirinius acted in that capacity. He had seen service earlier in the Near East as a junior, having fought in the campaign against the Homodanenses, a tribe in the Taurus Mountains from 10 to 7 B.C.; so that it would have been natural for him to have been posted again to the same area. And in fact Justin Martyr (c. 100- c. 165 A.D.)[8] records him as having presided over the census as *epitropos* (procurator). For what the fact is worth Thorley notes that on Dec. 25th of 2 B.C. there had been a series of planetary conjunctions involving Jupiter and that that planet would then have appeared due south of Jerusalem – over Bethlehem – and apparently stationary. Writing of the appearance of Halley's comet in 12 B.C. the historian Dio Cassius describes it as having 'stood over' the city of Rome in language which echoes Matthew's about the star of Bethlehem.

This is all a most attractive thesis. Its weakness is that Justin Martyr's paragraph may be merely a rough abridgement of Luke. The only writer to date the census specifically to 2/1 B.C. is Orosius, a late author (fl. 414-417 A.D.).[9] As a champion of Christianity he wrote a universal history with the genial theme that, whereas the human race had suffered numerous calamities in the Christian era, it had suffered more and greater in previous times.

Assuming that there was a population count in or about 2 B.C., we still have the improbability of Joseph having to travel the long distance from Nazareth to register. Yet it is also improbable that Luke would have dared to write of people having to leave their homes for the purpose if the whole ancient world had known this to be a fiction. And since it was normal for villagers to register in the chief town in their district, it is credible that some peasants had to journey as much as 15 miles to do so, and even camp or find lodging for a night. (Time might have been spent in queues!) Is it possible that Luke was correct in believing that Joseph had to make a long journey, but mistaken in supposing that his home was in Nazareth? Another incident in Luke's narrative suggests that it was not.

In Luke 1.39ff we read that Mary went on a visit to her cousin Elizabeth, who lived in the uplands of Judah, and whose husband, it is implied, was a priest in the temple at Jerusalem. Families were less mobile in ancient times; so that it would have been natural for Mary and her husband to have been living not far away from their relatives. They were within visiting distance. It seems a fair guess that Joseph's home was not actually in Bethlehem, but something like a day's journey away. Matthew, it should be noticed, never specifically says that Joseph lived in Bethlehem; and, after recounting his flight into Egypt, reports that he feared to return from there to the *region* of Judaea (Matt. 3.22).

Again, assuming that we can rely on Luke's tale about Zechariah with all its corroborative detail, Thorley accepts Martin's calculation that Zechariah would have been struck dumb, and John the Baptist conceived, in June of 3 B.C., and Jesus born in September of 2 B.C. This would fit far better with Luke's story of the shepherds; for the cold is severe in the upper levels of Palestine in winter. At Christmas Bethlehem is in the grip of frost; and all the flocks would have been in the folds by November.[10] Supposing the journey of the three wise men to have been not merely legendary, we need not assume that they arrived on the morning of Jesus' birth. Matthew says only, 'After Jesus had been born'; and Babylon was three months' journey away.

Luke's detail of the manger (*phatne*) sounds authentic. A feeding trough would have served well as an improvised cradle. But his further description of a birth in a stable is an unwarranted inference from this. Many of the homes of peasants would have had no clear division between the family's living quarters and the cattle stalls. And it is not so long ago that similar arrangements could be found in England. On the Rector of Epworth's glebe in the 1930s there stood a barn that contained both a kitchen range and a horse's stall with only an open doorway between. It was thought to have served for an Irish labourer in early Victorian times. Sermons of modern clerics about Jesus' being rejected even at his birth betray ignorance and false rhetoric.

Luke follows his account of Jesus' birth with that of his presentation in the temple at Jerusalem. This would seem at first sight to conflict with Matthew's tale of the massacre of the Holy Innocents and Joseph's flight into Egypt. If, however, the Magi did not arrive till mid-December there is room for the visit to the Temple in between (again, surely not from so far away as Nazareth). The lyrical outburst (the Nunc Dimittis) attributed to Simeon on this occasion, like those put into the mouths of Mary (the Magnificat) and Zechariah (the Benedictus), is probably of Luke's own composition, embellishing a traditional core. The ancient historians felt no qualms about composing what they thought were suitable speeches to grace an occasion if no actual record was available. Thucydides, for instance, makes the Athenian admiral answer point for point a harangue just made by his Corinthian opposite number some 20 miles away. Tacitus even presumes to improve on the emperor Claudius' Latin text. Luke would have been following the fashion, and, if so, did his work well. The canticles have graced the Church's services daily, both morning and evening.

With the Magi not arriving till mid-December, the traditional picture of their opening their treasures in the inn with the oxen standing by must be abandoned. The Holy Family would have returned home months before, along with the others registered. And Enoch Powell gives good reason for believing this section of Matthew's narrative (2.7–12) to be a late interpolation. Not only does the style of writing betray this, but, 'if the sorcerers could see and follow the star, so could Herod's police.' The swordsmen could have done their work without delay. There would have been no need for anyone to report back.

It does not follow that the journey of the Magi is completely fictional. It looks as if it might have come on top of rising Messianic expectations towards the end of Herod's reign. Ancient writers speak little directly of trends in thought and belief, and of the ebbs and flows in public opinion. We have to glean from casual references. One such is Josephus' report that some Pharisees promised the eunuch Bougoas that his ability to father children would be miraculously restored by a future king. This could only be the Messiah prophesied by Isaiah (56.3).[11] Philo Judaeus writes of the hope of a warrior Messiah about the same time.[12] Any such popular hopes would have been particularly unwelcome to Herod as a member of a usurping dynasty and as an Idumaean rather than a true Jew. The visit of the Magi would have made these vague speculations suddenly actual and precise. The increasingly suspicious and frantic monarch might well have decided to scotch the prospect at birth. He needed no chief priests to tell him where the Messiah was to be born. Anyone in Israel could have told him. But the scent was now three months old. A search among the surrounding villages was indicated, and, so as not to start the bird prematurely, this could be most naturally carried out by the Magi.

Led by a camel train it would, however, most certainly have been conspicuous and unusual, and provoked surmise in Joseph as to what was afoot. Descendants of David were later marked men for the Romans[13], and the registration would have provided Herod with a convenient list of targets. He may well have decided to remove from Herod's vicinity without the prompting of any dream. Their inquiries among the villagers may also have enlightened the Magi as to the character of the man who had begged their assistance, so that they too needed no dream from Heaven to decided to return 'by another way'.

This brings us to the Massacre of the Innocents; and we should reflect that, if the Nazis could exterminate the whole village of Oradour so as to liquidate a single Resistance fighter,

Herod would not have shrunk from the murder of all the young children in a district; nor would Matthew have dared to record an outrage that all his contemporaries knew to be a fiction.

There remains the vexed question of the Virgin Birth. It seems at first sight that this is incompatible with Jesus' being 'born of David's line' through Joseph. And there are signs that this was felt to be a difficulty in ancient times. The oldest surviving Semitic version of Matthew, found on Mount Sinai, explicitly speaks of Jesus as Joseph's own son. It reads: 'Joseph, to whom was betrothed Mary, a virgin, begot Jesus'; but our present recognised texts end the genealogy with, 'Jacob begot Joseph, the husband of Mary, of whom was born Jesus.' The suspicion arises that some editor amended Matthew's text to accord with approved theology.

However, Prof. Vermes has shown how, for first century Jews, Jesus could have been both Joseph's own son and born of a 'virgin mother'.[14] This is because the word 'virgin' had a different meaning for Jews and Gentiles. The Jews associated virginity, not with absence of sexual experience, but with inability to conceive. Thus Philo can write of Abraham's wife, Sarah, as having advanced 'from womanhood to virginity'. Both elderly women, who had passed the menopause, and young girls, who had not yet menstruated, were described in the same way.

The Palestinian Talmud[15] speaks of girls being married before puberty; and, since some ovulated before menstruation, cases occurred of their becoming pregnant. For Jews Jesus' might have been a virgin birth in this sense; and the Gospel writers, not being familiar with Jewish usage, might have felt obliged to adapt their narratives to suit the Gentile, and our modern, meaning of the word 'virgin'. Mary had to be reported as being already with child before her marriage.

Supposing Jesus to have been Joseph's own son, it is possible to discover a 'natural' basis for Luke's story of Mary's interview with the archangel Gabriel. To do so we must begin by removing from our minds images created by Italian art. This only equipped angels with wings for symbolic purposes, to distinguish them from human personages. The Greek *angelos* means simply 'messenger', and God can put his messages into human mouths, even into the mouths of people speaking the truth unawares. One such may have been one of Mary's friends or relatives.

Mary's song has often been described as a socialist and egalitarian document, expressing a preferential option for the poor. This prompts the speculation that Mary may herself have been a poor girl, with no prospect of a dowry to attract a young and wealthy suitor. And traditionally Joseph was many years her elder. So we may imagine a relative coming to her one day with words like these: 'Great news, Mary! You are going to get an offer of marriage; and the man's from the house of David. And with you too descended the same way, what a son you will have!' Years later, with her son's career before her, she would have recognised this as a message from God. Against this hypothesis is Jesus' denial that the Messiah had necessarily to be a descendant of David (Mark 12.35-37). If this was no trivial word-play, it indicates that he was himself aware that he had no such claim by birth.

There is another, darker, possibility, but one to be swiftly rejected. The Talmud[16] refers to Jesus as the son of a Roman soldier, Yeshu ben Pantera. This is no Latin name, but could be the name of a member of an auxiliary regiment, recruited, like the sepoys in British India, from one of the subject, less civilised peoples. They were commonly and prudently stationed away from their native countries; and we know how soldiers tend to behave in what they regard as enemy or occupied territory. It is credible enough that not a few Jewish girls suffered violence and rape. Nothing at all prevents a bastard from being a genius, even a religious genius. But hardly so the son of a rapist. Biologists now tell us that inherited genes determine moral, as well as physical, personality; and common observation accords with the theory. It passes belief that Jesus, whom Prof. Vermes describes as 'second to none in profundity of insight and grandeur of character', should have had such an origin. There is also a difficulty over dates. There would have been no Roman troops in Judaea or Galilee until after the census of 6 A.D. and the rising it provoked; and, if born, say, in 7 A.D., Jesus could not have been 'about thirty' (Luke 3.23) at the start of his mission.

Except in the birth narratives there is only one shred of evidence that Mary was pregnant before her marriage. This comes in one of Jesus' altercations with the Jews, who shout out, '*We* are not sons of a prostitute'.[17] The inference must be that Mary's condition was known to her neighbours, and that some of these were putting the worst construction upon the event. Joseph would then have had to make an agonizing choice. Annulment of the marriage contract would have been the normal expectation; and this could not have been done without public awareness. On the other hand Mary's character led him to believe in her essential innocence. He would have passed a mainly sleepless night, turning over the issues in his mind. Then in the morning he woke with his mind made up. He would face the sidelong looks and whispered comments, and take Mary as his bride. On this interpretation, the world's history has owed an immense, inestimable debt to Joseph.

We are left with three possibilities: (a) that Jesus was Joseph's own son, and his birth a virgin birth only in the ancient Jewish sense; (b) that Mary was made pregnant by rape; and (c) the traditional story of the Virgin birth.

Of course, there might have been a virgin birth in the Jewish sense also in (b) and (c).

Scholarship alone cannot decide between these versions; and further investigation is a task for theologians The question they have to address is whether it is only at his birth, and by means of a virgin birth, that God can take full possession of a man. If the answer is Yes, then a further question arises – why did not Jesus begin his mission and the revelation of his true nature until he was about thirty years of age? A need to act as breadwinner to a fatherless family does not quite occupy sufficient time. To the historian his baptism experience seems a more cardinal event than his birth.

CREDO

It is no more possible to decide definitely on the existence or otherwise of God than on the historicity of the Resurrection. The traditional philosophical proofs leave me cold. Years ago, before the BBC Third Programme became Radio 3, I dutifully listened to a debate on the question between Bertrand Russell and a leading Jesuit. I was little enlightened, but rather bemused by the continued logic-chopping on the distinction between contingent and necessary beings. I fancy that the bulk of my fellow men would have profited no more than I did. If God's existence can be proved only through philosophical reasoning, then Jesus' claim that divine truths have been revealed to the unlettered is vain indeed. There surely ought to be some homely and practical arguments to determine the issue one way or the other.

Only one philosophical argument impresses me – the logical requirement of a First Cause. It seems that Darwin's theory of evolution is now generally accepted. All living beings are descended from a common ancestor; and we humans, though very distantly and millions of times removed, are cousins to the dinosaurs. The multiplicity of living forms is due to the process of natural selection. But this is not a complete explanation of the present scene. Somewhere, at some time in the past, the process of evolution must have had a beginning. There must have been an initial impulse to set events in train. And that impulse can reasonably be ascribed to the hand of God.

The grand difficulty in persuading the non-believer is that

one is seeking for proof that there exists another dimension besides the obvious and familiar ones of space and time. These not only provide the environment for the life of the ordinary working man and woman but are also the conditions in which the scientist works. Fundamentally, however much assisted by sophisticated instruments, he is dealing only with the evidence of his five senses. Of course he works with more precision and exactitude than the ordinary person; but his thought and reasoning are still bounded by the limits of a three-dimensional world. Assuming, therefore, that the divine is the sphere of the timeless, it is a hard, virtually impossible, task to demonstrate the existence of God beyond doubt. And for the same reason it is hard to demonstrate the opposite. After the flight of the first Soviet astronauts the Kremlin triumphantly announced that they had discovered no God in space. Of course not. They were seeking in the wrong milieu. The declaration betrayed limited thinking.

To assume a fourth, timeless dimension for the divine, mankind's situation may be compared with that of some creatures dwelling upon, and confined to, the top, upturned surface of a cube, and without sight of its vertical sides. They could not easily imagine that the world was other than two-dimensional. The comparison is only a rough one, but it may serve to illustrate a point in argument. Just as these imaginary creatures would have difficulty in conceiving of a third dimension, so have we in conceiving of a fourth, of a world of the timeless. And it is in that sphere that God, if he exists, is to be found.

The above comparison is inexact in several ways. As related above (p. 79), there have been throughout history a select few individuals, the mystics in various faiths, who have claimed to have had direct, personal experience of the timeless. And there is, perhaps, a reference to this phenomenon by analogy in a line in T.S. Eliot's play *The Cocktail Party*.

The only man I ever met who could hear the cry of bats.

The cries of bats are too high-pitched for ordinary people to hear. They are simply inaudible to the mass of mankind, who might on the evidence of their senses doubt their existence. Similarly with the beatific vision enjoyed by the saints and mystics. But there is a difference. Scientists, with the aid of sophisticated apparatus, can assure us that a person who claims to have heard the cries of bats may be speaking literal truth: there really are those sounds in the air. But there is no human means of checking up on the reports of mystics. It is open to us individually whether we choose to credit them or not. If we do so, we have to adjust and rectify the comparison with the creatures on the cube. Their difficulty in seeing beyond the immediate surface of things is not so much caused by the nature of their environment as by a limitation in their eyesight, or by the way in which they have become habituated to focus.

The experiences of mystics may be discounted by sceptics as purely subjective. It may be said that, though they did indeed enjoy the perceptions they relate, these are not necessarily in contact with any reality. They may be no more than the product of a particular state of mind, a kind of intoxication induced by over-long, rapt prayer and contemplation. In one of his books Bertrand Russell warns us to beware of such states and compares them to the effects brought about by the drug mescalin. Under its influence a man once felt that he had plumbed the secret of the universe and, by a great effort of willpower, forewent its enjoyment, took up a piece of paper, and wrote it down. Awakened from his trance, he looked to see what he had written, and read the words 'An odour of petroleum pervades throughout'. Russell concludes that the insights of inspiration require to be verified afterwards by sober investigation.

We can, if so minded, depreciate and disparage the visions of saints and mystics in this way. But the witness of a more numerous minority of people is not so easily dismissed. These are those devout persons who, when questioned, profess an absolute and unquestioning belief in God's existence, but, when asked for the grounds of their faith, can produce no arguments to support it. Asked how they come to know that God exists, they answer that they simply know. Pressed further, they reply that this knowledge and faith is something given. One either has it or not.

This does not seem a very helpful answer for the sincere and genuine inquirer; but it does not mean that we should necessarily doubt their testimony. There may be degrees of spiritual awareness parallel to degrees and grades in musical ability. At the summit of that scale come the great composers like Mozart and Beethoven, who can pick up the score of a symphony and, reading from it, hear the sounds of all the instruments in imagination. A cathedral chorister can have a chord played to him and name its constituent notes, or sing a B double flat upon demand. At yet a lesser grade a member of a local church choir or of a choral society can read a line of music and sing it unaccompanied. Finally we come down to the tone-deaf.

Now the tone-deaf would not deny the achievements of their musical superiors. They are a fact of common knowledge and experience. The whole world is familiar with them, and no one would venture to doubt cathedral choristers' gifts. Yet when told by the devout that they have been granted a constant awareness of God's existence and support, many people are reluctant to believe them. Is this hesitancy logical?

To return to the comparison with the creatures on the top surface of a cube, we need to adapt the picture once again and imagine them accompanied by fellow beings who have been allowed a peep over the edge,[1] and who do in fact have an awareness of more than two dimensions, of depth as well as of length and breadth. And we have to imagine that there are features in the surface that suggest this – some slight bumps and depressions perhaps. This brings us to the Argument from Design.

The classical exposition of this was made by an eighteenth century divine, William Paley. He argued that, if anyone walking along the sea shore were to come upon a gold watch, the intricacy of its working would convince him that it was the product of some purposeful artificer. Its parts could not have come together as a result of random chance. Similarly with our familiar world. Not only the whole, but the various individual parts of it are so complex in structure that they could have come into that state only through the agency of a divine Creator.

Isaac Newton deployed the same argument concerning the cosmic sphere, pointing out that our planetary system is the result of an extremely nice balance of forces, and would break down if any of these were either greater or less. If the velocity of any planet were greater than it is, centrifugal force would carry it into outer space; and if its speed were slower, it would be attracted by, and fall into, the sun. And not only had the individual velocities to be precisely calculated. All had to be adjusted to the others. These facts argued the operation of a grand designer 'very well skilled in mechanics and geometry'. Similar thinking led Sir James Jeans to assert that God must be a superlative mathematician.

The same point has been made more recently by Professor Edward Harrison of the University of Massachusetts in the *Quarterly Journal of the Royal Astronomical Society*.[2] 'We do not know why natural qualities such as the strength of gravity, the speed of light, the electric charge on the electron and so on have the values they do. Yet the slightest variation of their values would result in a barren universe without stars or light. Why are they precisely adjusted to give rise to life?' There are, he says, two answers to this question. One is that a supreme being – God – designed the universe in just the form needed for life. Another possible answer is that our universe was created by comprehensible beings of superior intelligence living in another universe He comments that the first of these answers precludes further rational inquiry. But the second invites the query where these superior aliens evolved from, and what was *their* origin. We find ourselves going into an infinite regress.

It reminds one of the story of an Indian sage and his inquiring son. One day the boy asked his father why the world did not just topple down. 'Clever boy!' said the delighted father. 'Of course, the world *would* fall down, if that were all there is; but, fortunately, it is held up on the back of a great elephant.' The child beamed with enlightenment, but after a while grew thoughtful again and inquired, 'Yes, father; but what supports the elephant?' Overwhelmed with pleasure at the philosophic promise in one so young, the father replied, 'Shrewd again! You are not one to be satisfied with mere shallow solutions. Hear then the great mystery. The elephant itself stands upon the back of a large tortoise.' For a time the boy was satisfied. But after a minute a puzzled look came over his face. 'But what keeps up the tortoise?' he asked. Suddenly now the sage's expression changed. His brow grew dark and his eyes flashed fire. 'Impudent and presumptuous urchin!' he cried. Seek not to question the ancient wisdom of your race.' The superior aliens from another universe are really not much of an improvement on the tortoise. They are an explanation which of its nature invites further questioning.

Writing in *The Sunday Telegraph*,[3] Dr James Le Fanu declared himself increasingly persuaded by William Paley's arguments.

Consider the lung, with its surface area the size of a tennis court across which oxygen diffuses into the blood and carbon dioxide diffuses outwards – all compacted into the 6-litre capacity of the chest. Its tissue must be highly elastic to allow for expansion during inspiration, while the small air sacs are lined with a substance – surfactant – which prevents them from collapsing in on themselves at the end of expiration.

To preserve this delicate structure, air must first pass through the nose to be warmed on the way down and potentially noxious particles removed; this task is ably assisted by scavenger cells in the lungs and minute hairs in the airways whose rhythmic movements expel mucus upwards.

Beyond all this, the lung has a second function altogether, completely unrelated to respiration. It is a bellows that allows us to speak and sing, without which human society as we know it would be inconceivable.

The whole respiratory system is utterly dependent on each of its parts: a defect in just one and breathing becomes difficult or impossible. It is all or nothing, which is why I find it very difficult to believe that the lungs could ever have evolved by trial and error through the chance mutation of the many genes that control their development. Surely someone designed them to be the way they are?

This is an example of an intricate and complex mechanism within a single creature. More remarkable still are the instances of cooperative working between different species and organisms. The one most often cited is that of the pollination of flowers by bees and other insects. Clearly this is not any purpose aimed at by the bee. The bee's only object is the collection of nectar. The phenomenon suggests a third force, interested in the production of future plants and flowers.

Another example of cooperation not obviously purposed by either of the partners involved is that between the bracket fungus and the oak tree. One would suppose that the fungus was the equivalent of a vulture feeding upon dead carrion. Almost the opposite is true. What the fungus feeds upon is the dead, lifeless wood of the tree, the solid timber pillar in its heart. It is a kind of natural pruning which renders its host more resilient and stable. As a result an old hollow oak will remain standing when younger, apparently healthier specimens are blown over by a gale.[4]

The same phenomenon can be seen in the symbiosis of ants and acacia trees. The ants not only protect the tree's leaves from browsing insects but travel down the trunk and chew and destroy any seedlings of potential rivals and mutilate the buds and leaves of any other tree whose branches trespass into its territory. Their reward is the nectar obtained from the orange-coloured buds that grow from the tips of the leaflets.[5] Once more we have to ask ourselves how the partners were introduced to each other. It is not likely that the ants tried every tree in the world before fixing upon the acacia. If a thoughtful deity arranged the match, all could be understood. Otherwise a great deal of speculative ingenuity is called for. 'The simplest solutions are the best', said some crime novelist's detective.

All this, of course, still fails to convince agnostics. They may argue that all these examples illustrate are *effects*, not necessarily *ends*. It does not follow that because a number of factors combine to produce a certain result that that result has been purposed by any outside person or agency. The effect of the various constituent parts of the eye may be sight, and that of the various parts that compose the lung respiration; but there is no proof here that this was the outcome of any conscious plan or design.[6]

In pure logic this is a valid point; but the ordinary person will be more impressed by Dr Richard Dawkins' book *The Blind Watchmaker*. In it he sets out to demonstrate that some of the most complex organisms can have been evolved, as Darwin maintained, through the process of natural selection working upon random mutations, and that all our animal and vegetable world can be accounted for without assuming the agency of any Grand Designer.

His main point is that it is only the first, initial mutation that is random; and that, given that this is advantageous to the species involved, development from this will naturally be cumulative thanks to the influence of the mutated gene in one generation after another. 'Chance is a minor ingredient in the Darwinian recipe, but the most important ingredient is cumulative selection which is quintessentially *non*random.'[7] A distinguished scientist who worked in another field completely failed to understand this aspect of Darwin's theory. He fancied that it could be compared to an assertion that a high wind could blow through a scrap yard and miraculously assemble a Rolls Royce. This is an ignorant travesty of the evolutionist thesis. The essence of it is that so soon as an improvement has once appeared, others will follow in the course of time, in the same way that a succession of artist's touches will add up finally to a finished masterpiece.

We have also to take into account the effects of time, the aeons of ages that have passed since the origin of our Earth, some 4.5 billion years ago. Our minds are not adapted to working in, or envisaging, such numbers. But computers can do so. One of the newest chess computers can examine 10,000,000 positions per minute. Computers can, therefore, show us, by analogy, the large results of accumulated miniscule changes over great ages of time – rather in the same way that a modern camera film can be speeded up to show us a plant developing. And Richard Dawkins used his own to demonstrate how a few given factors fed into a computer programme can ultimately produce the most complex and intricate design structures. I have used the word 'analogy'; but this is inaccurate. The experiment is not merely an analogy. It is rather an illustration of the power of cumulative selection persisted in over a long period. We have to imagine the world's species evolving in a similar way.

In passing Dr Dawkins neatly demolishes Newton's argument from the planets. Of course their velocities are very nicely adjusted so as to maintain them in orbit. Those planets that were not moving at the necessary speed would either have spun off into outer space or been drawn into range of the Sun and burnt up! He also has an explanation for the existence of our lungs. All life is believed to have come from the seas, and he points out that some species of fish use the internal chamber of the mouth as a kind of crude proto-lung. This might have further evolved when some fish lived mainly in water but made brief forays out of it, to become the first amphibians. For them a mere 5% of a lung would have been a great advantage over having no lung at all. And similarly with eyes and wings. Even a small light-sensitive patch of skin could have its uses, in averting painful collisions for example; and flaps of skin growing out in the angles of joints could act as crude aerofoils to assist a small animal leaping from branch to branch of a tree. He does not go on to explain the uses of the lung for speech and song, but might perhaps have theorised that these developed from different types of grunt.

These are sound points. But they are not valid over the whole field. A mere inch of extra neck would not give the proto-giraffe a significant advantage over its fellows, nor a mere hint of a stripe provide much protective colouration to a zebra against a predatory lion. A few white hairs would not screen a polar bear from its intended prey. And a mere 5% of a penis would not mean a great advance in sexual reproduction. Minute quantities generally are ineffective, as we all know from the advice to dilute caustics inadvertently dropped upon the skin with water. A mere trace of strychnine is not poisonous at all but the only genuine tonic. The initial mutation has to be appreciable for the process of evolution to get started at all. I would not wish to be accused by Dr Dawkins of being a saltationist, believing in sudden leaps in animal development; but I do feel that there is a possibility that the original mutation which leads to the development of a new species may not be entirely random, but due to a decisive outside impulse. There is room here for a divine Creator giving an occasional touch on the tiller to keep the planned world development on course. A chess grandmaster can foresee the development of a selected variation for ten moves ahead on either side. It is, therefore, entirely reasonable to suppose that

Paley's Grand Designer could foresee and intend the evolution of the giraffe from its first gift of an extra two inches of neck. Continual interventions and guidance would not be needed.

The example of the 5% of a penis is not meant to be frivolous. Sexual reproduction is the main engine of the evolutionary process – as racehorse owners and dog fanciers discovered by practical experience. Indeed it was their conscious selective breeding for certain qualities that gave Charles Darwin the idea for his famous thesis. Without the mechanism of sexual reproduction evolution would be like a car engine attempting to run on a single cylinder. The tendency would be for the world to be populated by a series of clones, each a carbon copy of its single parent. So Dr Dawkins' exposition is incomplete without an account of the origins of sex. All he tells us is that 'sexual reproduction is a big theoretical puzzle for Darwinians'.[8] He treats of the preferences of female birds for certain kinds of plumage in males and how this can intensify the cumulative selection of certain features in a species. (Though one wonders how far the points he makes are valid for other genera. It is not common for the male to have to attract the female.) But on the larger question of how sexual reproduction itself originated he is silent.

It may be that a full account of its origin would have unduly enlarged the bulk of his book. It might demand a treatise to itself. But its absence deprives his exposition of a crucial and vital link. To be convinced that our world in all its complexity and multiplicity developed on Darwinian lines without the agency of a Grand Designer we require a plausible account of the origin of sex. It is not easy to imagine its arising from random chance.

What Dr Dawkins does do, in some rather demanding chapters, is to address the problem of how evolution, how life itself began. Briefly, he believes that the earliest entities with the power of self-reproduction were crystals. However, this still assumes the prior existence of the materials from which these first entities themselves arose. Perhaps Dr Dawkins prefers the theory of the Steady State to that of the Big Bang (I write here as a non-scientist). But if not, we are confronted again with the need of a First Cause.

Given the prior existence of the materials from which our present world evolved, Dr Dawkins' exposition of the process is persuasive. But his argument still falls short of complete success. He has shown how it is *possible* that the present multiplicity of plants and living creatures *may* have developed without the agency of a divine Creator. He has not proved that in fact it did so. He and the proponents of the Argument from Design stand much in the same case. Neither can they prove that a world of intricate organisms can have come into existence only through divine creation; nor can he prove that a divine Creator did not direct the process. His book may only have given us an insight into the Creator's methods. At the end of the inquiry we are faced with the question of ordinary probability. And there are some examples in Nature that agnostics must find particularly hard to account for on Darwinian lines.

One is that of the Worm Halipegus. This lives under the tongues of frogs, under which it lays its eggs. When these have hatched out, they pass through the frog's intestines into the water. Outside their host, they now have the appearance of hairy tennis balls, swim about, and penetrate into ram's horn snails. Once inside these second hosts, they hatch out and feed upon the snails' livers. Then, in the third stage of the life cycle, they leave the snails and lie on the bottom of a pond, withdrawn into their own tails. These tails grow things like flowers or ferns which attract the water flea or cyclops, which then eats them. The worms are then shot out into the mouth of the cyclops through a sort of hyaline tube. Next the cyclops in turn is eaten by dragon fly larvae with the worms curled up inside of it, and finally the dragon fly is caught and eaten in its turn by a frog. Then the worm pops out of the cyst and makes its way through the frog's guts and stomach up into its mouth; and there it makes its lodging under the frog's tongue for the whole cycle to be repeated. Thus the worm has four different lives and four different hosts. It is difficult to believe in a Darwinian explanation of the phenomenon. Dr Miriam Rothschild thinks the case argues for the existence of a God with a wry sense of humour.[9]

The same could be said of the means by which the Australian mistletoe is propagated. Its sticky seeds and berries are the main diet of the mistletoe bird. After being devoured, digested, and finally passed through its bowels and excreted, they still retain some residual stickiness; and this means that they do not part readily from the bird's posterior. So, to rid itself of them it sidles along a branch wiping its hindquarters clean. In this way the seeds are given firm lodgement on a new site on which to grow.[10] Obviously the mistletoe seeds need to have this adhesive quality. But what out-and-out evolutionists must explain is why that particular bird should feed exclusively on those particular seeds.

Still on the subject of defecation, the behaviour of foxes invites comment. After the cubs are born, the vixen has to lick their hindquarters so as to induce them to open their bowels. They would not otherwise develop normally. This practice seems to call from an explanation from Darwinians as to why other animals do not find the same necessity. The three examples might imply a Creator who does not view the natural processes in the same light as did the Victorians!

I fancy that evolutionists would have a harder time accounting for everything in the vegetable world than in the animal kingdom. Fully to demonstrate the workings of a benign Providence in this field would take a long book. A few striking examples must suffice. There is the fact that orchid seeds cannot be germinated and grown without the aid of a fungus, that certain trees, e.g. mountain ash seedlings in Australia, have need of a forest fire to give them opportunity to germinate, and that the bottlebrush is dependent on fire to provoke the shedding of its seed. Then there is the nice control of nectar in the aquilegia: enough to encourage humming birds to visit, but not so much as to deter them from passing on to neighbouring plants.[11] The defence mechanisms of leaves also invite reflection; how some are protected by spikes, others, like the common nettle, by stings, and others again by their poisonous quality. Fungi are particularly interesting. They are Nature's scavengers, disposing of dead plant tissues and even of Man's throwaway plastic. There seems to be an opportunity here for a new Darwin.

William Paley based his Argument from Design mainly upon the complexity of living forms and on how the various phenomena interlock. But there is another side as well. This stems from their aesthetically pleasing and beautiful character. Granted that the multitude of animal and vegetable life may have evolved through a process of natural selection, why should it so often be attractive to the eye? It is not just a mothering instinct that makes us delight in the sight of young animals; and others besides the artist Sir Alfred Munnings are entranced by the appearance of a racehorse. Young girls instinctively move to pick flowers. Why should all this be so?

One answer is the functionalist theory of art. This maintains that the products of good design are by the same token of aesthetic value. And there is great truth in this. Compare, for instance, the clean lines of a modern racing yacht with the crude contours of a Chinese junk. No amount of ornament could make the latter pleasing to the view. Or set photographs of pre-war cars beside those of today. The former look like boxes on wheels. A similar improvement in appearance has been effected by better design in small items like table knives and kettles. On these lines it could be argued that, if Darwinian natural selection can produce good, effective designs, these designs must automatically be beautiful.

The theory accounts for a great deal. But it does not seem to account for the beauty in natural scenery. Not that every landscape can attract the artist. The flatlands of Lincolnshire compare poorly with the Lakeland fells. But it can be claimed that Nature never falls below a certain level. Its greater charms inspired the poet Wordsworth with his pantheistic creed. He tells how, as he looked on Nature,

> I have felt
> A presence that disturbs me with the joy
> Of elevated thoughts; a sense sublime
> Of something far more deeply interfused,
> Whose dwelling is the light of setting suns,
> And the round ocean and the living air,
> And the blue sky, and in the mind of man:
> A motion and a spirit that impels
> All thinking things, all objects of all thought,
> And rolls through all things.

In passing one can note that few human constructions inspire the same feelings. Wordsworth would not have formulated his theory if he had lived in a concrete jungle, in the Liverpool 'Piggeries' or in the pre-war Gorbals. Assuming that Wordsworth's insight was valid, people who have to grow up and live without a regular view of the countryside are denied one of the essential hints of God's existence. Parks are not a complete substitute.

It is, however, only too easy to glory in a beauteous sunset and ignore the half-eaten rabbit at the edge of the wood. There seem to be flaws in the Design. 'Did he who made the lamb make thee?' asked Blake in his poem on the tiger. And tigers and sharks are not the only ruthless predators in the world. At a humbler level ladybirds feed on aphids, and blackbirds on worms. All around us we see a pattern of what are euphemistically called food chains, with one animal living upon the death of another. Nature red in tooth and claw is part and parcel of the system. And consideration of this aspect of animate nature provokes the question whether any moral Being could devise such arrangements. If moral goodness is an essential element in the conception of a divine Creator, then these facts cast serious doubt upon his existence.

In addition to these moral flaws, there are also technical ones to consider. One is the notorious evolutionary error in brain building whereby in arthropods/invertebrates (e.g. crabs and scorpions) their brains are built around their gullets, so that either their food passages are restricted or else the size and effectiveness of their brains.[12] Another instance is to be found in the eyes of plaice and soles. These fishes now lie on the sea bottom; but it looks as if this was not originally so and that one of their eyes had to be twisted round from the left to the right side. The flatfish is a similar case. The human eye also seems to have been designed back to front.[13] All the photocells in it point, not, as one might expect, towards the light, but away from it. These apparent errors in design suggest a God who is not all-wise.

Natural disasters, such as floods and earthquakes, are another problem for the theist. In a debate shown on television the former nun Karen Armstrong suggested that these manifestations of evil disproved the existence of God, or certainly of a good God. In reply the opposing theologians put up a feeble show. One ventured to suggest that disasters such as war and shipwreck had at least the merit of calling forth heroism. This is mere casuistry. Such palliation of suffering is an evasion of the main problem. 'Acts of God' like the hurricanes that so often devastate Florida can be explained only in two ways. Either they imply that God is not morally righteous – a frightening possibility glimpsed at by some tragedians – or that he is not all-powerful.

Speaking to the Church Assembly some years ago, Sir Richard Acland[14] boldly opted for the latter solution. If the spirit of God is indeed at work in history things should be constantly improving. We can see that they are not. We no longer have the Victorians' blithe and sanguine belief in inevitable progress. Beside Hitlerite Germany the Austro-Hungarian Empire seems an enlightened and progressive regime; and one cannot imagine the Tsars perpetrating such an act as Stalin's liquidation of the kulaks. Dictatorial governments in Africa and South America have shown a new brutality in oppression. Ours has been a doleful century. If, therefore, we believe in a God working wholly for good in the world, we must also believe in the existence of a counter force. Earlier ages personified this as the Devil, not so implausibly. To believe in such a being does not commit us to picturing him in our minds as a pantomime figure with hoofs and horns. The absurdity of the medieval conception need not lead us to the illogical conclusion that no opposing power exists.

Belief in a Devil is not, perhaps, completely incompatible with a faith in God's omnipotence. Orthodox believers might find a way out of the dilemma by claiming that while God is not in control of and dictating events every instant, he is nevertheless ultimately supreme. In the same way a master chess player cannot prescribe every move in the game, but is all the time in full command of the situation.

The Argument from Design is not conclusive. It cannot demonstrate the existence of God beyond all doubt, or that he is infallible. There are all those false starts in the process of evolution to be considered. Not only the dodo but many other species have died out. The sabre-toothed tiger and the mammoth no longer roam the earth, and not just because the climate would not suit them. Creation seems to have gone down blind alleys. And the argument of its nature does not prove that God is morally good or just. Indeed, so far as justice is concerned, the facts point the other way. Notoriously the just do not find their reward on Earth. Some theologians have argued from this that there must therefore be a Heaven so as to give them compensation. But this is to assume the very thing that needs to be proved, the existence of a just God.

Some evidence for this may be found in language, in the existence of the word 'ought'. We all have a sense of duty and an uncomfortable feeling when we act against it. And theists would argue that this has been implanted in us by God. It could, on the contrary, be maintained that it has been inculcated and drilled into us by parental and social pressures. Society sees that certain types of behaviour are a threat to it and accordingly imposes taboos: against murder, rape and theft. All the great historical codes prescribe in much the same way, impose a similar ethic. And the process has gone beyond the basics, so that we feel a twinge of guilt when contravening minor prohibitions, when parking cars in forbidden areas, for instance, or disposing of litter and rubbish where we should not. Public opinion enforces a certain ethos and tells us how we 'ought' to conduct ourselves.

But not all our uses of 'ought' can be accounted for in this way. Campaigners declared that veal calves 'ought' not to be shipped abroad in crates, or hens reared in batteries, or seal pups cudgelled to death, and, generally, that animals should not be maltreated. Where do these feelings of moral compunction come from? The theist would answer that they are divinely inspired, that they are the voice of God working within us. There is, though, the difficulty that not all nations seem to feel the same way on these issues; and even within the United Kingdom Scottish fishermen take a different view of seals from members of the Greenpeace organisation, just as farmers and countrymen do not regard foxes and badgers in the same light as compassionate townspeople.

Again we come back to uncertainty. In whichever direction we look, however we approach the question, there seems to be no reaching finality. The best brains in the world have been addressing it for centuries without reaching agreement. In the first century B.C. the Roman poet Lucretius argued that the world's many imperfections proved that it could not have been divinely created, large tracts being uninhabitable by the human race; and four centuries before him Greek physicists had constructed pictures of the universe in which there was no room for a god or gods. The question we have been considering has not arisen only recently. This lack of clear proof and agreement would be understandable if the issue were one of artistic tastes or political judgment or ethics as opposed to the exact sciences. But it is rather one of fact. And the question seems to arise why the philosophers and scientists have made no more progress than they have.

I suspect that this lack of conclusiveness is not accidental, and that God does not desire us to know for certain about his existence or otherwise, and believes that it is best for our moral state to remain in a measure of doubt. This is the condition of our freedom, of our having genuine and effective choice. If we knew for sure that God existed and was almighty we would not dare to oppose his will, any more than in the novel *Nineteen Eighty-Four* the inhabitants of the former United Kingdom dare oppose Big Brother. Not that God has any thought-police! And he does not wish us to believe that he has. Accordingly he has given us only hints of his existence. And the hints are even becoming fewer. The age of miracles (if it ever existed) is over; Charles Darwin has cast doubt upon the first chapters of Genesis; and churchmen no longer preach hell fire. The crutches to faith are being removed, one after another. We are being driven to a less naive and more adult spirituality. Doubt is designedly part of our condition.

What we can be sure of, however, is the existence of evil; and it almost seems to be increasing its menace. No previous century has seen a Holocaust, or the kind of 'ethnic cleansing' that has been perpetrated in the former Jugoslavia, or mass massacres on the scale of those done in Rwanda. There surely were not so many murders of women and girls in parkland before the war. And the deliberate sale of harmful drugs is now practised on an international scale. There seems to be a new cynicism in crime. Clearly the catalogue could be extended. There is much evidence of a moral relapse.

Moreover, this increase in ruthlessness in the human race comes at a time when increasingly powerful weapons are available to it. Since the discovery of the atomic bomb Man has had the power to destroy all life upon the planet; and that capacity is no longer confined to the great political powers. Nuclear proliferation is proceeding; and it may not be long before the deadly instrument falls into the hands of an irresponsible dictator or even of an extremist pressure group. This is the alarming background to the daily news that we mostly prefer not to think of; and the media do not often remind us of it. We are living very near the edge of a volcano.

We cannot rely upon political leaders to protect us from the peril. They are likely to be no more squeamish over methods or to be less swayed by narrow nationalist or sectional motives than private citizens. The commander of the British Falklands expedition was authorised to use a tactical nuclear weapon in case of need, and it was assumed that the Iraquis would employ chemical weapons in the Gulf War. The first steps to a disastrous escalation have already been taken. There is no knowing how reckless national governments may be in a situation of crisis. The only radical remedy for our perilous state is a revived and stronger morality. The human race needs urgently to turn over a new leaf. Having peeped over the edge of the abyss, we must draw back and mend our ways.

We thus arrive at a curious paradox. Whereas the presence of evil seems to cast doubt upon the existence of God, it also indicates the necessity of religion. For there is no other hope of an improved ethic. In theory one could be constructed and practised without any reference to God. An attempt to sketch one out was made by the Utilitarian philosophers. But the weakness of such systems was pointed out by Plato long ago. 'We cannot expect a whole nation to be philosophers.' Right conduct is largely a matter of habit, and habits have to be formed early in life. We really cannot imagine young Johnny engaging in moral discourses at the age of three.

All the great religions of the world beckon us in much the same direction. The moral codes they prescribe are similar. In no case can we be sure of the truth of their theological and metaphysical bases. But we have no time to plumb controversy to its depths, either individually or collectively. Events keep marching on, and we need to act. Are we, or are we not, on the side of the angels? Do we care for the future of the world? If we do, we must enrol in and support the appropriate organisation. Some words of W.H. Auden are appropriate:

> The stars are dead.
> The animals will not look.
> We are left alone with our Day. And
>   History to the defeated
> May say alas, but cannot help nor pardon.

Dubito, ergo credo. 'I doubt, therefore I believe.'

NOTES

Preface

1. Wilson, A.N. *Jesus* (Sinclair-Stevenson, 1992) p. 214.

The Background

1. Vermes, G. *The Religion of Jesus the Jew* (SCM) 1993 p. 37.
2. Josephus. *Antiquitates Judaeorum.* 17.42

The Evidence

1. Examination of the Greek text shows the borrowing to have been not so mechanical.
2. Enoch Powell, J. *The Evolution of the Gospel* (Yale) 1994. ad loc. *The Gospel of Thomas* (No. 33) also has 'bushel', which suggests that the corruption was early.
3. Mark 1.40-45; Matt. 8.1-4 (healing of leper); Mark 6.14-29; Matt. 14.1-12 (death of Baptist); Mark 5.21-43; Matt. 9.18-26 (healing of Jairus' daughter); Mark 5.1-20; Matt.8.28-34 (Gadarene swine); Mark 9.14-29 (the healing of the epileptic boy).
4. Robinson, J.A.T. *Redating the New Testament* (1959) p. 101.
5. *Historia Ecclesiae* 3.39.15 and 6.14.6ff.
6. See further in Mackendrick, P. *The Mute Stones Speak* (Methuen, London 1960).
7. Hist. Eccl. 3.39. 16.
8. McGregor Ross, H. *Thirty Essays on the Gospel of Thomas* (Element Books) 1990.
9. See further in Wilson, I. *Are These the Words of Jesus?* (Lennard Publishing, 1990) Chapter 7.

10. Ant. Jud. 18.63.

Mission and Messiahship
1. To compare very small things with great, I startled my aunt and uncle by showing a fascinated interest in the Elgin marbles when only seven and a half years old – perhaps after reading Kingsley's *Heroes*. This might, but did not, have pointed to a future Classical scholar.
2. Methodists may be reminded that John Wesley's mission began with his feeling his heart 'strangely warmed'.
3. Gore, C. *Jesus of Nazareth* (Thornton Butterworth 1929) p. 48.
4. G.Vermes (*Jesus the Jew* SCM 2nd ed. 1983 p. 147) points out that Mark. 8.31 follows on very awkwardly after the preceding verse. I think it fair to conclude that Mark 8.27-30 (the question of Jesus' identity) and Mark 8.31-33 (his prediction of his crucifixion) are accounts of separate incidents, brought together by Mark because of the related theme of Messiahship.
5. op. cit. pp. 160-191.
6. Robinson, J.A.T. *Redating the New Testament* (S.C.M. 1976).

The Miracles
1. op.cit. pp. 58-82.
2. op. cit. p. 63.
3. op. cit. p. 75.
4. Perrin, N. *Rediscovering the Teaching of Jesus* (S.C.M. 1967) p. 136f.
5. Vermes, op. cit. p. 63.
6. Breuer, op. cit.p. 288.
7. Lowther Clarke, W.K. *Concise Bible Commentary* (S.P.C.K. 1952) p. 371.
8. op. cit. p. 23.
9. *Sunday Telegraph* 4 Dec. 1994. It is just possible that Pastor Jeffries' visit to Sunderland took place during the General Strike

of 1926, when no newspapers were published. But I would not
then have been as much as seven years old – rather too young to
take an intelligent interest in such matters.

10. See further Marsh, F.B. *The Reign of the Emperor Tiberius*
(O.U.P. 1935) passim.

11. Yet Enoch Powell, op. cit. p. 137, regards the feeding both of
the five thousand and of the four thousand as allegorical.

12. Enoch Powell, op. cit. p. 142, suggests that the moral of the
case of the Syrophoenician woman is that Gentiles are to be
admitted to the Christian fellowship as junior partners.

13. Vermes, op. cit. p. 67.

14. See further Wilson, I. *Are These the Words of Jesus?* or, more
fully, Morton Smith, *The Secret Gospel* (Gollancz 1974). The text
is quoted p. 18 above.

15. In a letter discovered by Dr Morton Smith in 1958 and
quoted in I. Wilson, op. cit. p. 85, and at p. 18 above.

Jesus' Teaching

1. See Enoch Powell op.cit. p. 109.

2. ditto p. 154.

3. Jeremias, J. *The Parables of Jesus* (ET S.C.M. 6th edition 1963).
I am very greatly indebted to this book and to Perrin, N.
Rediscovering the Teaching of Jesus (1967) throughout this chapter.

4. Enoch Powell op. cit. p. 192.

5. ditto p. 193.

6. Pliny. *Epistulae* X. 96.

7. Perrin, N. op. cit. p. 103.

8. However, G. Vermes (*The Religion of Jesus the Jew* p. 147)
regards this last passage as an instance of the reworking of the
Gospels by the primitive Church.

9. ditto p. 22f.

10. ditto p. 23.

11. Enoch Powell op. cit. p. 82, suggests that 'hand' here may be
a euphemism for 'penis' as in several Semitic languages. But this

may be only an example of the thought of the latter 20th century.

12. This objection disappears if Enoch Powell is right in his conjectural substitution (p. 91) of 'the beasts' (*ta theria*) for 'the lilies' (*ta leilia*). In dictation the two words could easily have been confused.

13. See further in Vermes, G. op. cit. p. 183 with the references there given.

14. Sanders, E.P. *The Historical Figure of Jesus* (Penguin 1993) pp. 183ff.

15. Perrin, N. op. cit. pp. 164-199.

16. Robinson, J.A.T. op. cit. p. 73. On this subject we have to make two important distinctions: (a) between what Jesus said about himself to his disciples in private and what he said to the general public; and (b) between the period before his final entry into Jerusalem and that last week. On the face of it, his words at the healing of the paralytic (Mark 2.6-12) seem to make a large claim. But 'Your sins are forgiven you' would be a normal Jewish periphrasis for 'God has forgiven your sins'; since there was a taboo on mentioning God by name. The words 'The Son of Man has authority to forgive sins' must be regarded as an editorial addition. Otherwise Jesus could have been immediately arrested and tried for blasphemy.

The Trial

1. Schonfield, H.J. *The Passover Plot* (1966). esp. p. 44ff.

2. Winter, P. *On the Trial of Jesus* (Berlin 1961).

3. Brandon, S.F. *Jesus and the Zealots* (Manchester 1967).

4. op. cit. p. 308.

5. Josephus *Jewish War* II. 264 (p. 147 in Penguin translation) and Ant. Jud. 18.1-10, 23-5.

6. For a further criticism see D.R. Catchpole's chapter in Bammel, E. (ed.) *The Trial of Jesus*. 1970.

7. op. cit p. 140.

8. op. cit. p. 121.

9. But a more accurate translation here would be 'he was against allowing anyone etc.' *Ouk ephien* is to be regarded as a conative imperfect.

10. op. cit. p. 258.

11. ditto p. 260.

12. 21 July 1985.

13. op. cit. p. 214.

14. Josephus *Jewish War* VI 126 (Penguin tr. p. 347).

15. See p. 151 of J. Blinzler's chapter in Bammel op. cit., quoting from The Tractate Sanhedrin.

16. And the High Priest was later deposed for this (Joseph. *Ant. Jud.* 20.9.1).

17. Josephus. *Jewish War* II. 246 (Penguin tr. p. 146).

18. Cicero *Verrine Orations* passim and Pliny *Epistulae* II.11, X.81, X.110.

19. See Catchpole ap. Bammel p. 58f., where E. Lohse's claim of five infringements of rabbinic law is considered and criticised.

20. Josephus *Ant. Jud.* 18.4.3.

21. Bammel op. cit. p. 27.

22. Vermes, G. *The Religion of Jesus the Jew* p. 22ff.

23. Bowker, J. *Jesus and the Pharisees* pp. 43ff.

24. Ginsberg, A. *Ten Essays on Zionism and Judaism* (1922) p. 232.

25. Jeremias. op. cit. p. 202 f.

26. J.C. O'Neill ap. Bammel op. cit. p. 74.

27. Josephus. *Jewish War* II. 169-177 (Penguin p. 138).

28. Philo. *Leg. ad Gaium.* 301.

29. See William Horbury apud Bammel op. cit. p. 108.

30. op. cit. p. 152.

31. op. cit. p. 148.

32. op. cit. p. 93 ff.

33. op. cit. p. 95.

34. op. cit. p. 178 n. 21.

Resurrection?

1. In his chapter in Crossman, R.H. *The God that Failed* (1950).
2. See further Wilson, I. op. cit. p. 36, himself quoting from Jerome. *Of Illustrious Men*, a modernised translation after Robert M. Grant and David Noel Freedman. *The Secret Sayings of Jesus according to the Gospel of Thomas* (1960) (Harper Collins).
3. *Ant. Jud.* 20. 96.9.
4. Josephus Ant. 20.169.72 and B.J. 2.261.3 (Egyptian Jew), Ant. 17.10.5 and BJ. II.54. (Judas the Galilean), Ant. 17.271.2 and 14.159 (Hezekiah), BJ II. 417-24 (Menahem), BJ II. 447 (Eleazar).
5. See further Vermes, G. *Jesus the Jew* pp. 129 ff., esp. p. 134.
6. e.g. by John Hick in *The Myth of God Incarnate* ed. J. Hick pp. 168 ff.
7. At Cambridge in the Michaelmas Term of 1938.
8. Vermes, G. *The Religion of Jesus the Jew* passim.

What Manner of Man?

1. Odes III.3.12.
2. op. cit. p. 218.
3. Critical references in Paul's letters are: 2 Cor. 4.4, Col. 1.15, Phil. 2.6, Col. 1.20, 1 Cor. 15. 23 ff, 3. 23, 11, 3, Rom. 9.5, 2 Thess. 1.12.
4. e.g. Rom. 11.26, Gal. 1.4, Eph. 5.2, Eph. 5.23, 1 Thess. 1.10, Col. 2.13, 1.23.
5. By Serapion, Bishop of Antioch, in 190 A.D.
6. *Hymns Ancient and Modern* No. 315.
7. *Honest to God* p. 79.
8. For an analysis of the ancient thinking behind this custom see Glotz, G. *La Solidarité de la Famille en Droit Criminel de Grèce*, esp. the chapter entitled *L'Abandon Noxal*. The victim would be chased and pelted away with stones in symbolic disowning of it/him by the tribe.
9. Koestler. op. cit. p. 267.

10. Quick, O.C. *Gospel of the New World* p. 36. 11
11. Vermes. *Jesus the Jew* p. 224.

The Birth Narratives

1. See further Schürer-Vermes-Millar. *History of Israel* vol. i p. 403ff. for an almost definitive treatment of this whole question.
2. Tac. *Annals.* vi. 41.
3. Jos. *Ant.* 14.4.4.
4. Jos. *Jewish War* I. 187 (Penguin p. 52).
5. Appian. *Bell. Civ.* v. 75/319.
6. Vol. xxvi (1979). What might have fixed the date of Herod's death very precisely is the fact that a lunar eclipse occurred shortly before it. Unfortunately there was both a partial eclipse on 13 March 4 B.C. and a full one on 10 January 1 B.C.
7. Jos. *Ant.* 17.2.4.
8. Justin Martyr. *Apologia.* 1.34.9
9. Orosius. *History* vi. 22.6.
10. Dec. 25 was originally the festival of Mithras the Unconquered Sun, being the first winter day of noticeably longer light, but was adopted as Christ's birthday by the Church because of its irrepressible popularity – a clear case of 'if you can't beat 'em, join 'em'.
11. Jos. *Ant.* 17.2.4.
12. Philo. *Num.* 24.7.
13. Eusebius. *Hist. Eccl.* iii. 12, 19, 20, 32.14.
14. Vermes. *Jesus the Jew* pp. 213 ff.
15. Quoted by Vermes, pp. 219.
16. See further in Wilson, I. op. cit. p. 106f.
17. John 8.41. *Hemeis* is emphatic.

Credo

1. Readers of Plato's Republic will be reminded of the Allegory of the Cave and how one of the prisoners escapes for a while into the real world (Book VII. 514ff). Also very significant is a

passage in his Seventh Letter where he insists that the ultimate truths of his system cannot be communicated in logical discourse, but that the truth 'flares up suddenly in the soul'. This is typically the language of a mystic.

2. Reported in *The Times* 21 Aug, 1995.

3. *Sunday Telegraph* 4 Dec, 1994.

4. See Attenborough, D. *The Private Life of Plants* pp. 211ff.

5. idem p. 206ff.

6. See further in Stace op. cit. pp. 76ff.

7. Dawkins. op. cit. p. 49.

8. op. cit. p. 268.

9. In the television series, *The Seven Wonders of the World*.

10. Attenborough. op. cit. p. 230f.

11. idem. op. cit. pp. 222, 186, 188, 119 and 179.

12. See Koestler op. cit. p. 268f.

13. Dawkins. op. cit. p. 91f.

14. Richard Acland began his political life as a Liberal but became a socialist and formed the short-lived Common Wealth party. Putting his views into practice he donated his large West Country estate to the nation.

Books Mentioned in the Text

Ancient Authors
The texts of Josephus, Philo, the Younger Pliny and Eusebius have all been published in the Loeb Classical Library with facing translations in English. There is also an excellent English translation of Josephus' Jewish War in the Penguin Classics (G.A. Williamson's translation edited by E.M. Smallwood).

Modern Works
Attenborough, D. *The Private Life of Plants* (BBC 1995).
Bammel, E. (ed.) *The Trial of Jesus* (1970).
Bowker, J. *Jesus and the Pharisees* (Cambridge 1973).
Breuer, J. and Freud, S. *Studies in Hysteria.* (Pelican 1974).
Brandon, S.G.F. *Jesus and the Zealots* (Manchester 1967).
Clarke, W.K. Lowther. *Concise Bible Commentary* (S.P.C.K 1952).
Crossman, R.H.S (ed) *The God that Failed* (1950).
Dawkins, R. *The Blind Watchmaker* (Longman 1986).
Glotz, G. *La Solidarité de la Famille en Droit Criminel de Grèce.*
Gore, C. *Jesus of Nazareth* (O.U.P. 1929)
Hick, J. (ed) *The Myth of God Incarnate* (1977).
Jeremias, J. *The Parables of Jesus* (1963).
Hoskyns, E.C. and Davey, F.N. *The Riddle of the New Testament.*
Koestler, A. *The Ghost in the Machine* (Hutchinson 1967).
Marsh, F.B. *The Reign of the Emperor Tiberius* (O.U.P. 1935).
McGregor Ross, H. *Thirty Essays on the Gospel of Thomas* (Element Books 1990).
Paley, W. *Natural Theology* (Oxford 1828).

Powell, J. Enoch. *The Evolution of the Gospel* (Yale 1994).

Perrin, N. *Rediscovering the Teaching of Jesus* (1967).

Quick, O.C. *The Gospel of the New World* (1944).

Robinson, J.A.T. *Redating the New Testament.* (1976).

Sanders, E.P. *The Historical Figure of Jesus* (Allen Lane 1993).

Schonfield, H.J. *The Passover Plot* (1966).

Schürer, E., Vermes, G., Millar, F. *History of the Jewish People in the Age of Jesus Christ* 2 vols. (1973 and 1979).

Stace, W.T. *Religion and the Modern Mind* (Princeton 1952).

Vermes, G. *Jesus the Jew* (S.C.M. 1973).

Vermes, G. *The Religion of Jesus the Jew* (S.C.M. 1993).

Wilson, I. *Are These the Words of Jesus?* (Lennard 1990).

Wilson, A.N. *Jesus* (Sinclair-Stevenson 1992).

Winter, P. *On the Trial of Jesus* (Berlin 1961).